Aspects of
My Life

Also by Sam Zebba

The 39 Steps of Self-Division
A Structural Approach to the Depiction of Internal Conflict
In Six Famous Dramatic Works

Aspects of My Life

Selected Images

Sam Zebba

iUniverse, LLC
Bloomington

ASPECTS OF MY LIFE
SELECTED IMAGES

iUniverse books may be ordered through booksellers or by contacting:

iUniverse LLC
1663 Liberty Drive
Bloomington, IN 47403
www.iuniverse.com
1-800-Authors (1-800-288-4677)

ISBN: 978-1-4759-7472-0 (sc)
ISBN: 978-1-4759-7473-7 (ebk)

Library of Congress Control Number: 2013904052

Printed in the United States of America

iUniverse rev. date: 07/22/2013

Cover photo: Tessa Swade

To Tessa, my love

Preface

This little volume is not an autobiography in the regular sense, but rather a collection of separate reminiscences which, hopefully, stand as individual vignettes, while simultaneously revealing some aspects of the storyteller's life. It is neither a nuts and bolts account of a person's history, nor an amorphous bundle of disordered recollections. Rather, it is a little bit of both.

Throughout the years I have often been struck by the vast difference between life and art. Life, by and large, is random, haphazard, at times messy and jumbled. Art, on the other hand, is usually well thought out and finely engineered.

It is my hope that this offering will bring to light something of the randomness of life, yet also unveil a little of the writer's individuality, character and outlook.

The chapters are arranged in chronological order, yet the stories themselves, most of them having been written long after they occurred, are tempered by the hindsight gained through the passage of time and the accompanying age-acquired perspectives.

The book would never have happened were it not for Tessa Swade, my dear wife, who acted as motivator, critic, computer wizard, and English language expert. I am also deeply indebted (without knowing him) to Tim Berners-Lee, inventor of the Internet, whose innovation provided me with background information I would never have come across, even if I had taken copious notes throughout life, which I didn't. Thanks also to friend and art-photographer Gregory Rozansky, who took the best shots of my music activity in Israel. I am also indebted to several friends who permitted me to use their photographs in the book. Their names appear in the relevant photo captions. Lastly, my thanks go to the editorial staff of the publishers, who guided me through the intricacies of convention and style.

Many of the characters appearing in the book have remained close friends. But many other close friends I would have liked to write about are not included, for the simple reason that I did not find suitable story frames for them. To those I express my sincerest regrets and apologies. I love them, nevertheless.

Contents

1

The Good Earth

With my mother, Ventspils, 1925

In 1933, in the days of gathering storms in the Western world, I was transplanted, at the age of nine, from a distant, wintery, tranquil country on the Baltic Sea, Latvia, to a hot, barren, and contested land in the heart of the Levant, British Palestine. It was a move that saved me and my parents and those few family members who came with us or who managed to follow, from certain annihilation, first by the Soviet invasion of 1940, then by the Nazi Holocaust machine when Germany overran Latvia in 1941, and then again by the Soviet purge of those who were not communist enough when the Russians overran it a second time in 1944.

In Latvia my parents were Zionist oriented. I was sent to Hebrew kindergarten, and to the Hebrew Gymnasium in Riga, but I think the family was not Zionist to the extent of packing up and emigrating, had it not been for my aunt Fanny, my father's young sister, who at nineteen went to Palestine as a member of the Latvian delegation to the first *Maccabia* games, the international Jewish Olympics, 1931. When the games were over, Aunt Fanny refused to come back, and as the months went by my father was commissioned by my paternal grandfather to go out into that wilderness, that desert, and bring the girl home. "I rather think that I shall stay, and you will come here," Fanny told my father when he disembarked at Jaffa port, and she proved to be right. Within a few years not only we but most of my father's siblings came over, including one uncle with a young Christian German wife, and finally my grandparents themselves, Joseph and Esther (nee Brenner) Lipschitz of Ventspils (Windau), who managed years later to celebrate their golden wedding in the Promised Land.

In spite of my speaking the language, the transplantation was not easy, especially for my parents. My father's Hebrew was limited to what he had learnt from prayer books in *Heder*, and for my mother Hebrew was like Chinese. The apartment my father had arranged during his visit was not ready. There were four of us living in one rented room for months, my father was preoccupied with finding a means of livelihood, and the heat was oppressive. I started school immediately, although the school year had already begun, and on my very first day I was thrown out, I swear by no fault of mine. We were given a light meal in class, which consisted that day of several dates, a fruit I had never seen before. Clutching a particularly succulent one in my hand, perhaps too tightly, the pit suddenly shot out, and to my horror flew across the room directly into the principal's eye, the whole class breaking out in wild laughter. Not many years later I became quite proficient at target practice, at an air-rifle shooting gallery on the beach, but never again did I score such a bull's-eye.

The old world of my childhood, however, was lost forever. Of Latvia's Jewish population of 100,000, 70,000 were murdered, and the rest scattered all over the world, some of them to Palestine. In Riga, I remember our apartment on Pulkved Brieja iela, a big building on a corner, and also the modern one-family house we occupied for the year or two prior to our departure, in a residential area named Mezaparks (Kaiserwald). It was there that the famous Jewish historian Simon Dubnov lived, until shot by the Germans in 1941, having been too weak to be transported to the Rumbula forest outside Riga, where in two days, culminating on December 8, 1941, 25,000 Jews were massacred.

From an early age I spoke a number of languages. At home we spoke German; at school, Hebrew; with Maria the maid and my playmates in the street, Latvian; with my grandparents in the small town of Ventspils (Windau), Yiddish; and with some of our relatives, Russian, which I didn't know well. My parents spoke Russian when they didn't want me to understand, and when they suspected my proximity, the codeword they used was *"patom"* ("later"), followed by silence, which only prompted me to learn the language all the more and to improve my eavesdropping techniques.

'Mother' in German was 'Mamma,' and in Russian 'Mahma,' the two having quite different connotations—the first strict, the latter forgiving. 'Mamaah,' in German, was something else altogether. It referred to my maternal grandmother Johanna Sebba (nee Eliasson) in Liepaja (Libau), and implied respect for a proud and revered lady. Indeed, she had raised nine children, and her apartment on the ground floor of a three-storey building served as the family hub, especially during holidays, when my mother would take me there for Passover. Although not religious, Mamaah had enough dishes for every occasion. There were four complete sets of twenty four, including silverware and pots and pans, one *Fleishig* (for food containing meat), one *Milkhig* (for milk and milk products), one *Pessachdike Fleishig*, and one *Pessachdike Milkhig* (same, but used during Passover week only). The hallway in the house had a particular smell, emanating from the garden in the back, where along the fence tomatoes for home use were grown. Ever since I could remember, Mamaah seldom smiled, and always wore black. She had been a widow since 1915, and as the first-born of her daughter Rosa, I was the third male grandchild named after my deceased grandfather, Samuel. Families were huge in those days, and there were others named Sam among my mother's sixty three first cousins. Politeness and modesty were the order of the day at that time. Sisters-in-law forever addressed one another with the respectful "*Sie*" ('they' in German), and any aunt bringing a home baked cake from her kitchen was almost obliged to announce, "Today it didn't come out so well."

At age four or five I made the discovery that, I believe, separates humans from other living beings: the knowledge that one day we must die. I was walking in the street with my mother hand in hand, when a very old and wrinkled woman dressed in black passed us. I remember feeling an intense fright, and I said, "Oh, I don't want to die." "You won't." said my mother soothingly. "Doesn't everybody?" I wondered. "No," she said, "some die, some don't." This seemed to me an evasion, perhaps rather an admission, a confirmation of my suspicion. It was also a lesson that for the sake of living at peace with oneself, it is all right to bend the truth a little, although even then I noticed that for my mother, bending the truth was distasteful, and indeed she didn't do it well at all.

At age five or six, I was taken to my first music lesson. The piano teacher, a Germanic professor oddly named Schubert, sent me to the window and told me to face the heavy, dark-green, antique-smelling curtain. He played two notes on the piano and asked me how many notes he was playing. I said two. He played three notes and I said three. He turned to my mother, and said he'd take me on. When I came to my first lesson, I went straight to the ancient curtain and turned my back on him. "What are you doing there?" he shouted. I didn't know that to learn the piano you needed to be seated at one. Shyly I came forward toward him.

Summers, my parents used to rent a *dacha* near the sea in the Riga Bay area. Getting there was an adventure in itself. Our *dacha* came unfurnished, and for the two or three summers I can remember, a Latvian truck driver named Rudzit was hired to transport basic household furnishings from our Riga apartment to the *dacha*. I was allowed to ride with Rudzit in the cabin, while the family would come by train. Rudzit and I quickly became great friends, and he allowed me to sit in the back among the cargo, enjoying the breeze and observing the world from up high. Once there, I loved the beach and wading in the cold Baltic waters, but no less did I love to listen to one of the Novik girls who played the piano in the *dacha* next door. Although no more than twelve at the time, she played very well and practiced a lot. Through listening to her play, I got to know Beethoven's Piano Sonata No. 8 in C minor, op. 13, the *Pathetique,* better than any of his thirty two Piano Sonatas.

At age seven or eight I found a thrilling place to hang out in the afternoons: a small music store owned by my father's young cousin Leah Brenner. It was on Riga's elegant Brivibas ('liberty,' formerly Alexander) Blvd, and it was full of treasures, both music and records. The piano music I saw there was inexhaustible, and of the records I particularly liked the coloratura soprano Amelita Galli-Curci, including the very sound of her name. I also liked Leah herself with her big eyes and friendly smile, only in her early twenties and already a shop owner.

Luckily for Mamaah, she died before the Holocaust began, and was spared the tragedy. My cousin Hilda was shot with her baby while hiding in a cellar with many others. The baby cried and the Germans heard it and came down and killed all of them. My uncle Ludwig Sebba was sent by the Russians to a Gulag in Siberia, and quickly perished. Remarkably, his wife Paula Sebba (nee Licht), sent to a different prison in Siberia, survived for years before she died of cold and hunger. My uncle Meyer Sebba vanished without a trace. Another uncle, my father's brother Kaufman Lipschitz, was killed in Kuldiga (Goldingen), with his wife and two children. Leah herself escaped to New York, but her father, my father's uncle Bernard Brenner, was dispatched to Siberia and soon died there, and the fate of his wife Jennie remains unknown. My uncle Ede Sebba fled all the way to Montevideo before joining us in Palestine. My cousin

Sam Sebba escaped to Shanghai and became a policeman, but had to run again in the 1948 Chinese revolution. I do not know what happened to my aunt Tsila Sebba (nee Friedlander), Hilda's mother, nor to the piano-playing Novik girl and her family, nor to all the other Jewish people I had known in Latvia.

So in a way, by coming to Palestine I was born a second time. Here I liked the colorful medieval pantaloons and the Turkish red hats, the fezzes, worn by the Arabs in nearby Jaffa. I liked their guttural language and their expressive way of talking. They were exotic and romantic to me, and I think my curiosity for other cultures in my later years was aroused then. Little did I understand that the Arabs were unhappy with us Westerners interfering with their way of life, and that we were, and had been since the beginning of the 'Return' in the 1880's, on a mutually irreconcilable collision course.

Tel-Aviv was small at the time, and we lived near the beach. Often the whole family would descend to the sea before school for a swim in the mild Mediterranean, and I watched with awe the long camel caravans on the water's edge, each camel tied to the one in front like wagons of a train, the locomotive being an Arab seated comfortably on a small donkey, singing to himself an ornamented Eastern melody in barely audible high-pitched tones. The caravans were bringing building materials from Jaffa for the construction of the Reading electric power station north of Tel-Aviv.

Accustomed perhaps to occupying a *dacha* in the summer months, my parents once rented a small stone house at the edge of Talpiot, a suburb of Jerusalem situated on the mountainous water-divide between the Mediterranean and the Jordan valley. The view east, in the days before pollution, with the Dead Sea below, was breathtaking. Arab women from

Bethlehem dressed in Biblical garb came by to sell fresh fruit and eggs to the houses in our neighborhood. The front of our house faced an enormous, empty area occupied by the mandatory British forces. Although too far away to be seen, the unit closest to us was the army band, which we could clearly hear. Incessantly rehearsing the same few marching tunes, the precision they achieved was remarkable. I could listen to them for hours, realizing that the way to perfection was arduous, and that nothing could be accomplished without effort and commitment.

My parents' good friends, the Freudenheims, perhaps distantly related, had come to Palestine a few years before us from Germany and had brought their children's non-Jewish governess, Hanna Walter, with them. She was a shapely dark-haired, light-skinned young woman, who seemed to feel at home in her new environment. She had a boyfriend in Jerusalem, and once she took me to meet him at the beautiful Jerusalem YMCA. His name was Najeeb Mansour, and for the first time I met a different kind of Arab, one I had not seen before. He seemed entirely Westernized, wore a well tailored suit, and spoke English and German. I liked him a lot, but to my regret I never saw him again, either because Hanna preferred to meet him without me, or perhaps because the romance had come to an end.

One summer the family went on a holiday to Cyprus. A sea voyage to Limassol and a long drive on dirt roads to the mountains brought us to the village of Platres, covered in green, with rivulets of water everywhere. The hotel owner was appropriately named Mr. Cypriotis, and unforgettable were the English style breakfast meals served there, consisting of bacon, fried eggs, and pork sausages, which I loved. My parents had given me and my cousin Kaly a Kodak box camera, and awakened in both of us a passion for photography. Every day we ran down the hill to the village center to develop exposed film and get new stock. In later years, in the Herzliya Gymnasium we both attended, we became somewhat notorious, photographing our teachers unawares in class, and selling the pictures to classmates and other pupils throughout the school. The operation became a notable success, and to ease our conscience we framed all the photos we had taken and stealthily hung the humorous collection in the teachers' room.

My first piano teacher in the new country was Dora Rosolio, sister of the young Zionist leader Dr. Haim Arlosoroff, whose mysterious murder in 1933 has remained unsolved to this day. Dora and her husband Werner became friendly with my parents, and were exceedingly kind to us new arrivals. Werner, born in Germany, had trained as a concert pianist, but while fighting in the German Army in WW1 he was shot in the arm, and had to abandon his chosen career. I hit it off with the two Rosolio boys, Shaul, a year older than I, and Dani, two years younger. Music was a central part of the Rosolio household, Shaul studying the cello, Dani the violin, and within a short time we became, if not a notable Piano Trio, surely one of the youngest around. Shaul became my closest friend throughout adolescence, and remained so until his untimely death many decades later. His calm demeanor in moments of stress was incredible. Once, in our late teens during maneuvers in the Haganah, something exploded near the two of us. A white cloud obscured him completely and only when it cleared did we see Shaul in flames leaping away and falling to the ground. Stunned momentarily by the sight, it was he who yelled, "Cover me with sand," and thus we extinguished the fire on his clothes and body. In spite of the burns he suffered and a long recovery, he became a successful police officer, studied law, and eventually served as the country's chief of police and later as ambassador. Dani, also seriously wounded a few years later in the War of Independence, joined a kibbutz, became a member of Parliament and a central figure in the Labor movement.

One day, when I was about twelve, Dora told me that she had decided to transfer me to a real piano teacher, herself being but a "rhythm tutor." Dora had at that time given birth to a girl, Noa, and was perhaps busy with the new addition to her family. I thus fell into the domain of Ilona Vincze Krauss, a recently arrived young Hungarian woman who soon became the doyenne of piano teachers in the country. Her husband, Laszlo Vincze, a doctor of law and an excellent cellist who later joined the Israel Philharmonic, taught Ilona's piano pupils theory and harmony, which fascinated me even more than playing the piano. I was naturally pleased with the promotion, but I loved Dora deeply and missed her very much. My favorite Bar Mitzvah present, at age thirteen, was the one I got from the Rosolios: an edition of Beethoven's thirty two Piano Sonatas, in one volume.

One of the core events in those days was the establishment, in 1936, of the Palestine Orchestra (later the Israel Philharmonic), a world-class musical body rarely seen before, let alone in these parts. Founded by the great violinist and visionary Bronislav Huberman, he brought leading Jewish musicians from Europe to form the orchestra, thus saving them from the approaching Holocaust. No less of a world figure than Arturo Toscanini came to conduct the opening concert. I was miserable when my parents insisted that I was too young to be taken to the evening's gala concert. But at school that morning, the principal,

Mordecai Vilensky, of the ill-famed date-pit incident, went through every classroom and asked certain pupils to come with him. Among those collected were Shaul and Dani Rosolio, Haim Taub, myself, and a few others. "We are going to the dress rehearsal," the principal announced, and only then did we realize the common link between us. Mordecai (we addressed all the teachers by their first name) knew exactly who, in the whole school, was studying music. Needless to say, attending that rehearsal was an unforgettable experience, and over lunch at home I could already report to my parents my impressions of what they would hear that evening.

My musical education was enhanced also by my new aunt Essi, whom my bachelor uncle Ede (the one who had escaped to Montevideo before coming to Palestine) married at that time. Essi had come from a musical family in Finland, and played the piano. As an extracurricular activity, she played four hands with me, and it was through her that I got to know most of the Beethoven symphonies, long before I could read orchestra scores.

Another informal musical input came from our relative Max Shamir (originally Sheftelowitz, also from Riga), who was half of the respected graphic team, the Shamir Brothers, designers of the emblem of the State of Israel and many of its postal stamps and bank notes. Max played the piano well, and had a liking for light music. I became enamored of one of his heroes, the British pianist of the Savoy Havana Band, Billy Mayerl, whose celebrated piano single *Hollyhock* I would play at the slightest provocation.

But I was also attracted to the 19th century romantic greats, especially when more than one art form was involved. We had several volumes of German *Lieder* at home, and the combination of poetry and song fascinated me. I loved Franz Schubert's *Der Leiermann* (The Hurdy-Gurdy Man), from his famed cycle *Die Winterreise*, in which he underscored Wilhelm Mueller's evocation of loneliness, cold, and dejection by the use of repetitive empty fifths in the bass voices, a device which surely caused raised eyebrows among harmony experts of the day. Another *Lied* I loved dearly was Robert Schumann's *Die beiden Grenadiere* (The Two Grenadiers), based on the bitingly sarcastic ballad by Heinrich Heine, of two French soldiers returning defeated from Russia. One of them, mortally wounded, asks his comrade to carry his corpse back to French soil so that if the emperor should come riding over his grave, he would rise out of the earth and resume the defense of the beaten emperor. Schumann used a most appropriate musical theme, no less sarcastic in its effect, for the song's ending: the French national anthem, the Marseillaise.

The arrival in Palestine, during the dark days of WW2, of the "Tehran Children" was a unifying national event. In an unprecedented humanitarian gesture, the British administration allowed several hundred Jewish orphans from Poland, stranded in Tehran on their flight from the advancing Nazis, to enter Palestine. My mother and her good friend Mrs. Gornitzky took it upon themselves to care for one Tehran child, a young piano prodigy named Janek, who became a member of our household, practicing long hours on our piano. He could play the most difficult passages of a Liszt or Chopin Sonata at twice the required speed, but he never played a movement from start to finish, and he never spoke about his past. When asked about his family, he would answer laconically in broken German, "*Er getot*," ("he dead"). Eventually Janek left Palestine for America, but he never recovered from the demons chasing him. Decades later I visited him in New York, where he was still practicing the same difficult passages while being supported by the city's welfare department. But on my next visit a few years later, I found that he had died, probably by his own hand.

At age thirteen or fourteen, Shaul Rosolio, my cousin Kaly, and myself spent a summer on a kibbutz. We worked half-days, in exchange for room and board. Housed in a huge packing plant of citrus fruit, empty off-season, we were each given a bed. Against one wall were stacked empty wooden packing boxes, and we had great fun arranging them in one corner of the 'hangar' to form cozy rooms and basic furniture. Working on a kibbutz was a national priority in those days, and in high school later on, up to a month of each school year was spent on a kibbutz. That summer was a major step in my transplantation process.

At fifteen-and-a-half I was sworn into the youth wing of the Haganah. One of my first jobs was to transfer a revolver from one address to another on my bicycle. The weapon was wrapped in a newspaper and I carried the package in one hand while cycling. To this day I remember the spot on crowded Allenby Street, where the mishap occurred: it was dusk, and I bumped with my bike, of all people, into a policeman. The impact tore a hole in the newspaper and the barrel protruded out of the package fully exposed. Had it been a British policeman, my fate would have been sealed. But the fellow was a local recruit and spoke Hebrew. He scolded me at length for my carelessness on the road, when suddenly, noticing the barrel, he stopped short, looked around furtively, and said to me. "Go, go, only be more careful."

We had a telephone at home, quite a rarity in those days, and when my section leader in the Haganah, *Tsherra*, a cool-headed

and efficient fellow, would call, and my mother answered, all
he would ever say to her was a terse "*Et* Shmuel" (To Shmuel).
He would never speak more than those two words to her, and
my mother became rather annoyed at his "lack of manners."
Despite her reservations, many years later *Tsherra* became
Israel's sixth Chief of Staff, 1961–1963. His full name was Zvi
Tzur, and one of his first actions was to appoint Major General
Yitzhak Rabin as his deputy.

One of the most impressive senior Haganah people I got to
know and respect was our camp commander Shmuel Lipowitz.
Paradoxically, the most endearing memory I have of him is
not so much his command of the art of war, as his rendering
of an Arab love song he used to sing around the occasional
campfire, *Razahly, Yah Razahly.* He sang it beautifully, with all
the Arabic lyrics, and I felt those moments of poetry were
perhaps a reminder to us that the enemy was just as human
as we were.

Truthfully, I was not entirely happy with the oath I had taken
to be ready to lay down my life, if necessary, for a nation several
thousand years old. Was there no oath of allegiance required
to life itself, older by several billion years? Nevertheless, I took
my duties seriously. Unwillingly, I even laid music to rest, and
for the remainder of my youth became a soldier, part-time
until matriculation, full-time afterwards. My transplantation
was thus complete.

More than half a century later, when Latvia regained its
independence, it fell to me to visit the land of my lost childhood,
actually twice. Once, with the last of my living uncles, my father's
youngest sibling Shimon, on a 'roots' trip, and once, within
the same year, when invited to lead the Liepaja Symphony
Orchestra in concert. Both visits were distressing experiences.

Of the Jewish community there was not a trace left. In Riga, at the Hebrew Gymnasium, converted now into a residential building, a youngish German innocently asked who I was looking for. He was the head of the Goethe Institute in Latvia, and had no idea he was living in what was once the center of Jewish education in the country. The sight of what was left of the unfenced Jewish cemetery in Ventspils was particularly agonizing. Broken tombstones were scattered on the ground, some of them inscribed with the name Sebba with dates from the turn of the century, "Why are the graves empty?" I asked the guide. "They were pilfered in search of gold in the teeth of the dead," was the answer.

The Latvians themselves did not fare much better during the long Soviet rule. In Liepaja I described to a local guide Mamaah's house, the three-storey building, but I had no idea where it would be. The guide promptly took me there. The house looked exactly as I had remembered it, and was still the only three-storey building in the area. It had served as the KGB headquarters throughout Soviet rule, I was told, and was now used by the Latvian Police. Alone, I walked in, soon to be asked to leave, but not before tasting that long-familiar smell of Granny's hallway. Back in Riga, before departure, I rang the bell at the Pulkved Brieja apartment where we had lived. A Russian woman opened a narrow crack, protected by several ill-fitting door chains. I explained I was a tourist, and that I had lived here long ago, before leaving Latvia for Israel. "No," she said, "I have lived here for forty five years," and was about to shut the door. "Wait," I pleaded, "I left Latvia sixty five years ago." The woman was undecided. "The kitchen is to the left, the bath over there," I hastened to inform her, "I was six years old then." She paused in uncertainty, but finally started to release the chains. What I saw inside was pitiful. Three families lived there now, padlocks across most doors, twelve human beings sharing one kitchen, one bath, one toilet. In Mezaparks I found the house we had lived in, although at first I was a bit uncertain about the place. I was accompanied by my cousin Yoram Shamir ("son of the Shamir Brothers," as he liked to call himself) who declared triumphantly, "This is the house, no doubt about it," and waved the sketch of the house he had asked me to draw, as I remembered it from childhood, on a paper napkin during breakfast that morning. Approaching the cement post at the driveway, I was suddenly transported to that unforgettable day when Rudzit slowly backed the loaded truck out of the driveway, this time carrying all our belongings in a large wooden crate designed by Uncle Shimon, the newly graduated civil engineer in the family. In spite of Rudzit's caution, when reaching the gate area, the truck hit the post, sending it flying into the street, felling Uncle Shimon, who now lay prostrate and motionless on the ground. With Rudzit's help, we carried the unconscious Shimon into the empty house and laid him down on the floor, clueless as to what to do next. Luckily, Shimon's injuries were not very serious. Bandaged and limping, he was able to join us the next day, as planned, on our voyage to Palestine.

Now, if Yoram and I could detect a sign of breakage on that post, or if the post was newer than, or different from, other posts in the fence, this would settle the issue. Indeed, in true Sherlock Holmes and Dr. Watson fashion, we discovered a marked crack at the post's base, suggesting that it had been severed and plastered back into place. Soon several people came out of the house, which had hitherto seemed locked up, to see what we were doing loitering at their fence. Upon hearing our story, they invited us in and we spent a pleasant morning together. The house, they told us, had been a mental asylum during Soviet days and was returned to its legal owners only a year before our visit. Two middle-aged couples, children of the original owners, were painting and renewing the house by themselves, and expected the work to last another year or two. They were hoping that the beautiful daughter of one of the brothers might get an entry visa to the USA. Latvia offered them no hope.

My father, who in 1924 had earned a doctorate from Frankfurt University in Economics and Political Science, became a successful businessman in Israel, active in a number of charities and public affairs. He was an outspoken secularist, a 'man of the world,' but he never forgot his roots in the *stetl*. At family gatherings he sometimes sang old Jewish songs that were close to his heart. One of his favorites, and mine too, was the Yiddish song 'Soll Zeyn,' penned by Joseph Papiernikov (1897–1993). Here is the first stanza:

> Soll zeyn, az ikh boi in der Luft meyne Schlesser
> Soll zeyn, az meyn Gott iz in ganzen nit do
> In Troim iz mir besser, in Troim iz mir heller
> In Troim iz der Himmel noch bloier wie bloi

And in free translation:

> Be it, that in the air I build my castles
> Be it that my God is not present at all
> In my dream it is better, in my dream it is brighter
> In my dream, the sky is more blue than blue

These words conveyed perhaps more than anything else the essence of the lost world that was, and is no more.

British Army March in Talpiot

Razahly Yah Razahly

Early years in Latvia...

...and in Palestine

2

A Star Is Born

The first time I met pianist Pnina Salzman was in 1939. She had just returned with her mother from Paris, where she had spent seven years studying with such luminaries as Alfred Cortot, Magda Tagliaferro, and Arthur Rubinstein. She was now seventeen or eighteen, and the first recital she played upon returning home was at the house of Werner and Dora Rosolio in Tel-Aviv. I was a few years younger than Pnina, and considered myself lucky to be among the guests. It was an evening that changed the musical landscape of the country.

It was the first time I had been so close to a performer, and I was amazed that someone could play so well. I was overwhelmed by her artistry, her phrasing, her technical ability, her memory. I was also impressed by her seriousness of manner, her refined deportment, her sculpting the air at the end of a lyrical phrase. No less was I impressed by her mother who, although hiding in the shadows, constantly fretted over her daughter. I realized that to become a young virtuoso, besides talent and will-power, a full-time, dedicated, and ambitious mother was vital. Mrs. Salzman had the necessary credentials. Having enjoyed a musical education before coming to Palestine, Miss Kostelanetz (her maiden name) was a close relation to the

Russian-born Andre Kostelanetz, the popular conductor and arranger in the USA in the first half of the 20th century. She was also an accredited kindergarten teacher.

Already that evening Pnina displayed the very stage personality she maintained throughout life. Her long black hair, combed straight down, and her deadpan face, except for a momentary grimace while acknowledging applause, became her trade mark. She had the trappings of a star, besides being one, and for the next sixty six years, until her death in 2006 at eighty four, she was the uncontested First Lady of the Piano in Israel.

The recital at the Rosolios also marked the beginning of a lifelong association between Pnina and me. For many years I enjoyed turning pages for her in chamber music recitals, sometimes traveling with her Israel Piano Trio or her Israel Piano Quartet throughout the country. "Don't look at my fingers," she insisted, as though that could cause them to get entangled with one another and set off mistakes. But by concentrating on her page, I got to know the works they played, and usually never missed a cue. Once, however, at the old Tel Aviv Museum on Rothschild Blvd, before the present Museum was built, there was a mishap. I had to get up from my seat near the piano and turn one page for the violinist. To my disgrace, in my eagerness I stumbled over the foot of the violinist's music stand and it, with all his music, went flying across the floor, causing a few gasps in the audience. If only the earth would open up and swallow me, I thought. Astoundingly, the musicians played on. The show must go on, I understood at once. Calmly I collected the pages off the floor, set up the stand, and returned to my piano duties just in time to turn the next page for Pnina. I'm glad to say I wasn't fired.

Pnina was the first Israeli pianist who toured the world, playing with major orchestras under such renowned conductors as Georg Solti, Carlo Maria Giulini, Erich Leinsdorf, Antal Doráti, Paul Paray, Malcolm Sargent, Igor Markevitch, Charles Munch, Zubin Mehta, and many others. In 1963 she was the first Israeli to play in the USSR, and in 1994 the first Israeli pianist invited to play in China. In 2006 she was awarded the Israel Prize.

While in Cairo in the mid 1940's on a concert tour with the Israel Philharmonic (then still the Palestine Orchestra), she met her future husband Igal Weissman, who decided to make his home with her in Israel. Originally from Russia, the Weissmans had lived in Turkish Palestine already before WW1, but in 1915, like many others, they had gone to Egypt to avoid being under Turkish rule during the war, and had flourished there.

Tragically, Pnina's younger brother Yair, a promising violinist who had also studied in Paris, was killed in the War of Independence. Shot and wounded, but unable to be evacuated, he died in the field without medical attention. When a child was born to the young couple, the baby was named Yaira, after her fallen uncle.

The Weissmans lived in a large roof apartment in a prime residential area in Tel-Aviv. Tastefully furnished, the huge living room was a veritable museum of mementos and paintings of Pnina, as befits a personage of her stature. Once, at a small dinner party on the veranda, Igal preparing grilled steaks on the fire, I sat next to US Ambassador to Israel Walworth Barbour. We sat on light aluminum chairs equipped with hand rests. It was an excellent and ample meal, and when at the end the guests stood up, Barbour's chair (he was a rather bulky gentleman) went up with him. I tried to pull the chair off him, but from one side it would not come off. Next to Barbour on the other side sat Israel's Foreign Minister Abba Eban, who joined in the effort to free him, and we finally managed to release the ambassador from his restraints. It took a super-human effort to suppress breaking out into laughter, so hilarious was the scene. But Pnina, poker-faced as though nothing out of the ordinary was happening, helped gloss over the episode.

Pnina had a wide repertoire, and constantly enriched it with works of Israeli composers, many of whom dedicated their works to her. She premiered and often presented works by such leading musicians as Paul Ben-Haim, Marc Lavry, and Mordecai Seter. Shortly after the Six-Day War, Pnina was approached by an Arab family in Ramallah to coach their piano-playing daughter. It involved Pnina traveling to Ramallah to give the lesson, a condition she accepted. The lesson turned out to include a sumptuous lunch and a comfortable sofa in a cool, darkened room for a siesta. After several visits, Pnina suggested that I take up the contact, and indeed my proposal to meet the young lady was accepted. We arranged to get together in Jerusalem's American Colony Hotel, the acknowledged meeting place for parties from both sides. At the appointed time two elegant ladies entered, mother and daughter, both as though straight from a Paris fashion magazine. They spoke perfect English, and during the ensuing conversation the idea came up to arrange an evening at my house in Tel-Aviv, to which like-minded people would be invited to engage in a dialogue outside of political lines. We parted with a spark of hope that evening. Sadly, the plan came to naught, as soon afterwards it transpired that the young lady "got married to a Jordanian and moved to live in Amman."

Pnina was an adjudicator in the Arthur Rubinstein International Piano Competition for over three decades, and she served as adjudicator on numerous other international competitions. I had the honor of serving on the competition's Artistic Committee, whose job it was to select competition participants from among several hundred applications. Astoundingly, Pnina was familiar with almost every applicant, no matter from what country, having met or heard so many young artists on her travels.

Despite her façade, Pnina was a fun-loving musician at heart. She famously recorded the Brahms Waltzes op. 39 for four hands with Arie Vardi, and her dead-pan expression was even more effective when, with Bracha Eden, Arie Vardi, and Alexander Tamir she was videoed at a public concert playing the now classic version of Larignac's uproarious *Galop Marche* for one piano and eight hands, without cracking a smile. Although never a big talker, her sense of humor was as sharp as a knife, and her chamber music partners would often be distracted to tears in rehearsal, laughing at her funny remarks, always delivered with a straight face.

Igal, who had served in the British Army during WW2, was a devoted horseman. An aristocratic type, tall and handsome, riding fitted his image. Once he had an accident with his horse, and I visited him in hospital. One leg was in a cast and suspended high in the air. In a field somewhere, Igal told me, the horse had fallen and crushed his leg. Reminiscent of Yair's fate, Pnina's fallen brother, Igal was unable to move and too far to call for help. The horse eventually got to its feet and waited, but when Igal remained on the ground, it wandered back to the stables where, upon seeing a horse without its rider, a search party was quickly organized. The horse led the party back to where Igal was lying, and thus saved him. On another occasion Igal joined me one summer on my sailboat for several weeks in the

Greek islands. He was a gentleman through and through, quiet, considerate, and self-possessed.

Shortly after my father died, in 1981, I organized an evening in his memory at the Tel-Aviv Museum, where several of his friends and associates were to speak. When Pnina heard of it, she promptly and generously offered to play a musical interlude, providing the assembly with a solemn and distinguished air. I shall never forget her kind gesture.

A long-time Professor of Piano and Head of the Piano Department at the Music Academy of Tel-Aviv University, Pnina continued to perform solo and in chamber music recitals. At one such occasion, I met Pnina's mother for the last time. "I am at Ichilov Hospital," she said in her heavy, hoarse voice. "What, Pnina will play a concert, and I shall not be there?" she demanded, and added more intimately, "I got out of bed, took my street clothes from the locker, went to the bathroom to change, and walked to the elevators. After the concert I shall go back, and no one will have noticed I was gone."

When I heard that Igal had died, I spoke to Pnina on her intercom. "I'm downstairs, would you like me to come up?" "Oh, thanks," she said, "but I think I would rather remain alone." "Of course," I said. They did have an unusually good marriage, I thought as I walked away, even though their interests differed markedly. When Pnina herself passed away, I realized I had lost a close, intimate friend, and a loyal Israeli who preferred to live in this country even though a residence abroad might have advanced her international status. She preferred to live close to her family and friends, and to play in kibbutzim and for soldiers at the front lines. At her funeral, while eulogies praised her lifetime achievements, I remembered vividly and with longing that amazing young girl at the Rosolios with the straight black hair, who had played so wonderfully and never cracked a smile.

Pnina smiling, circa 1970

3

A Fallen Heroine Revisited

Bracha Fuld, circa 1945 (photo source unknown)

Bracha Fuld was born in Berlin on December 26, 1926, the second daughter to Lotte and Luther Fuld, both parents being members of affluent, assimilated Jewish families resident in Germany for several generations. Luther Fuld, an artillery officer in World War I, named his daughter Barbara, after St. Barbara, the patron saint of the German artillery corps, in which he had served for four years during the war.

Already in childhood Barbara demonstrated a high sense of motivation. She learnt to read and write by herself, aided by her older sister's notebooks, and in school she distinguished herself both in studies and in sports, earning numerous prizes. Hitler's rise to power in 1933, however, brought a sudden change to the family's contented life style. At school Barbara was subjected to anti-Semitic incidents, and at home disagreement rose between the parents as to Barbara's continued education. Barbara's mother favored a Jewish school, but her father objected. Eventually Barbara did transfer to a Jewish school, while Petra, the older girl, was sent off to an uncle in the USA.

The infamous *Kristallnacht* of November 9, 1938 caused Barbara's father such a loss of faith in the Germany he prized that he committed suicide. Barbara was hastily lifted out of Germany by a family friend in Holland, and Mother Lotte, now a refugee, met up with her daughter in England, where she enrolled Barbara at a boarding school near London. Having failed, however, to acquire a work permit in Britain, Lotte was forced to leave the country, and decided to seek immigration for herself and Barbara to Palestine, where she had relatives. This came about in the spring of 1939, when Barbara was twelve. Lotte found a small apartment in Tel-Aviv, on 13 Pinsker Street, and opened a modest yet attractive candy shop nearby. Barbara entered the Balfour High School in Tel-Aviv, and changed her name to *Bracha*, 'blessing' in Hebrew.

Bracha soon excelled at school, and became known for her diligence. She took a liking to literature and music, and became interested in social activities. She first joined the Scouts movement, then the Habonim, and finally the Haganah, where she served as courier. After graduation from high school in 1944, she enlisted, together with several of her schoolmates, into the Palmach, forerunner of the Israel Defense Forces. She was assigned to H Company and stationed in kibbutz Kiryat Anavim near Jerusalem.

In the kibbutz Bracha met and fell in love with Gideon Pelly, the kibbutz's eldest son. Gideon, however, was soon caught by the British while on maneuvers near Beit Ha'aravah, and sentenced to seven years imprisonment. Bracha continued her relationship with Gideon by correspondence and by visits to Jerusalem's Russian Square prison, where Gideon was being held. (Gideon, released two years later when the British left Palestine, was killed in action almost immediately in the Battle of the Castel near Jerusalem). Continuing her underground activity, Bracha was sent to a course for sports instructors, and after that to a strenuous course for section commanders at Juara in the mountains of Ephraim, where again she became a high achiever.

After completing this course, Bracha was transferred to the Palmach E Company, then under CO Raffi Weinberg, and was given command of a section of women soldiers in kibbutz Givat Hayim. She soon won a reputation for being a thorough and exacting officer, a '*yekke*,' earning approval and admiration. Bracha demanded much of those under her command, but she demanded even more of herself. To her close friends she confided her aspirations to study medicine in the USA, but she refrained from taking steps toward this goal in the prevailing situation.

On the night of March 24, 1946, Bracha took part in the planned landing of the refugee ship *Orde Wingate*, which was to come ashore right on the beachfront of Tel-Aviv. The strategy of trouncing the British blockade by landing survivors on desolate beaches had become increasingly ineffective, and the present stratagem—a well-planned, large-scale operation—was designed to quickly conceal the new arrivals among the citizenry, in case the British were in close pursuit. Actually, Bracha was not assigned to participate in the action at all, but she and her friend, Carmela Cassa, insisted on joining the force, begging Raffi Weinberg for permission. Raffi refused at first, as the landing this time was to be defended, if need be, by the use of fire. Eventually Raffi agreed to ask Yigal Allon, Palmach's Commander in Chief, who came by for a last-minute inspection. When the latter consented, Bracha, as a section leader in the platoon of Danny Mass, set out on what was to become her last mission.

Approaching territorial waters, after a clandestine two-week voyage from Italy, the tiny vessel *Wingate*, carrying 238 Holocaust survivors, was apprehended by the British Navy, and diverted directly to Atlit, the detention camp near Haifa, where illegal immigrants were being incarcerated. Bracha and her section of six fighters had been assigned to hold a gun position on a balcony of an old building at 21 Marmorek Street in Tel-Aviv. Marmorek was but a few hundred yards away from the British military base Sarona, from where British troops, if ordered to thwart the landing, would be expected to approach. Tragically, the signal to abort the operation, which by now was called off, did not reach Bracha. When a British armored vehicle did approach from Sarona, Bracha, following previous orders, opened fire. In the exchange, Bracha was shot and badly wounded. Three of her fighters were trapped and arrested, and Bracha herself, bleeding heavily, was taken to Jaffa for interrogation. Only after a few hours was she transferred to a hospital, where she soon died.

Bracha was buried in the Haganah sector at the Nahlat Yitzhak cemetery. In spite of police efforts to keep the funeral unannounced, word of mouth spread quickly and crowds swarmed to the burial, intensifying the call for bringing an end to British rule. Bracha was survived by her mother and by her sister Petra, who had remained in the USA.

The press gave wide coverage to that night's events, and the Haganah publication *Hachomah* issued a proclamation in her memory, with her picture. The renowned poet Nathan Alterman wrote a moving obituary in his *Seventh Column*, and dedicated a cycle of poems to Bracha's memory in his collection *The Pidgeons' Town*. In October 1946 an illegal immigrant ship carrying over eight hundred refugees sailed to Palestine under the name *Bracha Fuld.* Sadly, it too was apprehended by the British and its human cargo sent to detention in Cyprus, Atlit having by now become overcrowded. A street in Tel-Aviv, near the place where Bracha was killed, was named after her. In 1958 Bracha's family established the Bracha Fuld Memorial Collection at the National Library of the Hebrew University on Mount Scopus. More recently, a well-researched biography of Bracha appeared in Hebrew, (Sari Gal, *Bracha Fuld*, Sifriat Poalim, Tel-Aviv, 1999). In March 2005 Tel-Aviv Municipality organized a memorial evening for Bracha, in the presence of the mayor and other dignitaries, the first of a planned annual event honoring past "Heroines of Tel-Aviv." It took place on the fifty-ninth anniversary of Bracha's death.

I attended that solemn memorial, which inevitably brought back memories of the Bracha Fuld I knew. I had met her in 1942 in the Gadna, the Haganah's youth troops where, my being two years her senior and a freshly graduated section leader, Bracha was one of my new recruits. She was a stunning, nimble girl, dark-haired with determined, steely blue eyes. In an enigmatic way, she seemed both engaging and distant at the same time. She was an excellent young soldier, always reporting in on time, always neatly dressed, always following instructions meticulously. It was by chance that I discovered she was taking piano lessons with one of the country's top teachers.

Our military ways eventually parted, but I remained in contact with Bracha and with her mother. Lotte Fuld was a cultured woman, whose change of fortune from her previous life could in no way be detected. Her shop and her home were small replicas of an urbanity not often seen in our parts.

I liked Bracha a lot, admiring her for her beauty and her quiet fortitude. It was only after she had finished high school and had joined the Palmach that she opened her heart to me a little, perhaps because I was now far away, and revealing herself in writing might have been easier for her. In any event, there developed between us an unexpected and candid correspondence, which lasted until her untimely death.

The memorial evening I attended, and the memories it evoked, moved me to find out more about Bracha than I actually knew. I was not sure what exactly I was looking for, but the ease, nowadays, of pressing a few buttons and becoming an armchair investigator made the temptation irresistible. Opening the Palmach website, of which I had not been aware before, there appeared under Bracha's name a concise summary of her life and death. It was, to my knowledge, accurate, and I have cited it almost verbatim in the first part of this essay. Eager for more personal data, however, I remembered Bracha's sister Petra. Now in her mid-eighties, I found her in Detroit, but too ailing to respond. Her son David, born almost on the day Bracha died, knew next to nothing of his heroine aunt. Nevertheless he offered to establish a Bracha Fuld website in English, an idea to which I promptly pledged my assistance. The project, however, quickly came to naught. I never heard from him again.

My thoughts turned to Bracha's letters from the Palmach, which reached me in a British Army camp in the Egyptian desert. Although seemingly well-adjusted to her role as an underground fighter, inwardly Bracha was not at peace with herself. In her letters she questioned her ability to fit wholeheartedly into the national struggle, and at times had forebodings as to its possible outcome. Gideon, her acknowledged boyfriend, was not her ideal choice, lacking the poise and the aspirations she longed for, but now that he was in prison she felt duty-bound to remain loyal. Toward the end, her letters became increasingly despondent. Her last letter to me arrived a few weeks after her death had become known even at my distant outpost. It was dated one day before her fatal encounter.

Ever since, I have kept these confessions strictly confidential. It would have been unbecoming to disrobe a national icon of the steadfastness and the tenacity expected of a fallen hero. Only once did I make an exception to this self-imposed rule. When I returned after the war, I gave the letters to Bracha's mother. Actually, at her request, I added a handwritten translation into English, as Lotte had never really mastered the Hebrew language. She bore her cruel fate with supreme dignity, yet in many ways she remained an outsider in Israel, and eventually moved to the USA. I stayed in contact with her for the rest of her life, until her death of a stroke, in 1968.

Delving into the Palmach archives again, the circumstances of Bracha's death had not ceased to perturb me. How was it that the order to call off the operation did not reach Bracha? Was no signal sent out to her at all, or had a messenger on his run been detained or arrested because of the imposed curfew? One report claimed that a runner on a motorcycle did arrive at the post. If this was so, was his message ambiguous? Did Bracha doubt the order's authenticity? In a larger context, why was a forward, pivotal position assigned such a small, isolated detachment? And why was it established by no more than a general's dismissive, last-minute acquiescence? In a more personal sense, was Bracha perhaps too quick on the trigger? Was she, the exemplary soldier, following orders too well? Did her mood of gloom impair her natural instinct for survival? Was there, perhaps, deep down in her soul in a moment of crisis, a dark horrific impulse inherited from her father?

It was the uselessness of Bracha's death that made her fall so unbearable. The sad truth was that Bracha died for nothing. On a different Palmach entry describing the Wingate action, I was shocked to find an item no less outrageous. Here it said that residents of the house, disturbed by the commotion caused by the motorcyclist's arrival, called the police. Twenty minutes later the armored vehicle was there. Was Bracha, then, simply betrayed by some spineless turncoat, cut down by the police as an armed thug or common criminal?

Some fifteen years after Bracha's fall, Lotte told me of Bracha's secret love affair with a British officer. This was preposterous to me, to say the least, and I refused to believe it. Was Lotte, vanquished by her grief, beginning to lose her mind?

Nevertheless I was gradually drawn into this myth. Whenever Lotte spoke of the affair, it seemed to bring her a sense of solace. Knowing of my occasional penchant for writing, she encouraged me to sketch out her version of the story. In her sorrow, haunted perhaps by remorse or even guilt for having come to this country at all, Lotte must have been desperate to accord her troubled, short-lived child a speck of happiness. I myself longed to rectify the futility of Bracha's sacrifice, if only in my imagination. I accepted the challenge. Considering the circumstances, the implausible liaison began to acquire in my mind a measure of credibility. After all, cases like this were not totally unknown at the time, even if looked down upon. In the narrative I created, with a bit of poetic license, the landing operation does succeed, and although the young heroine dies, she does not die in vain: her death facilitates the landing. The lovers, however, being of opposite sides, must be doomed. The man leading the assault on the fated gun position is, unwittingly, none other than the girl's lover.

The little story, written as it was for a readership of one, seemed strangely to fulfill its purpose. Lotte was comforted by the fabrication, and I laid the piece to rest. Nevertheless, throughout the years to come, I often wondered why Lotte had chosen to fancy such an inelegant, gratuitous tale. I never found a reasonable explanation unless, of course, there was an element of truth in it. But nowhere was there a hint to be found. Lotte herself had told me of having destroyed any evidence of the affair left in her apartment, for fear of exposing the man in case of a house search by the British, not an uncommon occurrence in those days. The biographer Sari Gal, to whom I introduced myself at the memorial evening, was appalled by my inappropriate inquiry, and I felt ashamed for having asked. An elderly lady I met at the Philharmonic not long afterwards turned out to be none other than Carmela Cassa, Bracha's tentmate in the Palmach. I delicately questioned her on this issue. She was rather dismayed. No way that this yarn could be true, she declared.

A few months after the memorial, while idly clicking Bracha's name one night into a yet untried search engine, I was startled to come upon an item "Bracha–Heroine of Israel." It appeared as a chapter in a book oddly titled *The World's 30 Greatest Women Spies,* by one Kurt Singer. The publisher was Wilfred Funk, New York, 1951. Within seconds messages went out to all major booksellers on the net. As I feared, the book was out of print, but an obscure supplier somewhere shipped me an old used copy.

What I read was staggering. It was the Bracha Fuld saga, complete as we know it, yet it centered on the elusive love story I thought was but a figment of Lotte's tormented imagination. This version, however, had a bold and epic twist, as implied in the book's title: the Englishman, an officer at the infamous Russian Compound prison, whom Bracha had met while visiting Gideon, becoming "one of Israel's most valuable helpers in her war of independence." Was Bracha's love story with the Englishman, if indeed it occurred at all, merely a ploy to obtain intelligence? Was Bracha then, as the book claimed, a successful Israeli spy?

Who was this Kurt Singer anyway? In no time I had him pinned down. Born in Vienna in 1911, he became an anti-Nazi activist in Germany, escaped to Sweden and on to the USA, worked as a spy for the Allies, and wrote biographies (one of them on President Lyndon Johnson) and spy stories. There was no date of death given, neither were his whereabouts. Could he still be alive? I started to look for him, frantically I may say, considering his age at the time (it was end of 2005). Desperately

I wanted to know how he came to the story, what sources he used, who that mysterious Englishman really was. Singer, alas, was not to be found. It was only through the kindness of an aging couple in Germany, Gerhard and Ingrid Zwerenz, well-known old-time anti-Nazi writers I had found on the trail, that I finally obtained the e-mail of Kurtillo, as he was known among his friends. A bizarre thought struck me suddenly. Did Lotte know Singer? Was she his source? Yet even if so, would the old spy master have taken on a mother's tale without thorough verification? How authentic was his writing? How much of it was fiction? Sadly, Kurt Singer was, of all places, in Santa Barbara, California, on his deathbed. My questions to him were never answered. A month later I learnt that Singer had passed away, aged ninety four. He died on December 26, 2005, on Bracha's birthday. Gerhard Zwerenz, who had helped me locate Singer, sent me the obituary he had written in a German paper about his old friend *Kurtillo*.

My chase had thus come to a dead end, and in any case Singer would have been under no obligation to reveal his sources to me, much less to disclose the Englishman's identity. The one question that could still be posed was whether Lotte and Kurt had actually known each other, and even so a positive answer would be no more than subject to speculation. I renewed contact with Bracha's nephew David in Detroit, whose mother Petra was still alive, and the answer I received was yes, Lotte had known Singer for many years.

In the absence of evidence to the contrary, I think it would be reasonable to assume that Singer wrote the story based on Lotte's representation alone, and that he did so, much as I myself had done, to console the heart of a woman weeping for her slain child. Lotte lived out her life honorably and decorously, and the extraordinary fantasy, almost certainly conjured up by her, may well have helped her, paradoxically, to preserve her sanity. Ultimately, the true cost of a national icon is borne by a grieving mother, and the price is infinite and immeasurable.

4

Suez

On His Majesty's Service, 1945

"**N**ex!" shouts the Egyptian impatiently behind the counter, and slaps the palm of his hand noisily onto the surface, "What you want?" He is all business, and his defiant eyes say it all: 'the morning break is short, the canteen is full. No time for long selections, you Englishman.' Not that there is much of a choice anyway. It is either tea or lemonade.

No sooner has the customer uttered his wish than the

Egyptian, at the top of his voice, hollers a long *"uahad shaay"* ("one tea") or *"uahad lamoun"* ("one lemonade") to no one in particular. Completing the financial side of the transaction, the palm of his hand hits the counter again, and another "Nex!" is hurled at the queue. The scream of the order, however, does not go unnoticed. A terrified little boy, the Egyptian's son or his child laborer, deftly fills his master's commands, though never winning as much as a glance of recognition from his irate boss.

When my turn in the queue comes up, I save the Egyptian the dialogue and yell out, in my best guttural Arabic, an extended "Uahad lamoun," followed by a loud slap of the right change onto the counter. The Egyptian is flustered, but not for long. Calmly he turns to the kid, jerks his head in my direction and says almost in a whisper, "Ha'ateenhu uahad lamoun," ("pass him a lemonade").

Except for the wooden shack of the NAAFI canteen, and the tin shower-house built on a cement floor, with running water for one hour in the early morning, the rest of the camp is tents and trucks. The camp is surrounded by barbed wire, although inside and out, as far as the eye can see, the landscape is the same: flat empty desert. Not the graceful sand undulations one might expect, but a hardened, depleted patch of naked planet.

We are in the Land of Goshen, a strip of Egypt not far from the ramshackle town of Suez, which marks the southern end of the famed canal that bears the town's name. Surgically separating Africa from Asia, yet strategically linking the Mediterranean to the Red Sea, and thus to the Far East beyond, this masterpiece of French ingenuity and English diplomacy ensures that the sun, as the saying goes, never sets on the British Empire.

Uninhabitable as the land is, compelling events took place here at the dawn of history. Goshen, according to the Book of Exodus, is where the Israelites, led by Moses, crossed the Red Sea from Egypt to the Promised Land, from bondage to freedom. Miraculously, the Israelites walked across the waters safely on dry land, while the Egyptians, chasing them in their chariots, got clogged down in the rising waters and were drowned. Since childhood I had been familiar, like any Jewish kid, with this dramatic yet implausible tale, recited anew every year in great wonderment on Passover night. Growing up, however, one wondered whether the myth was a product of pure imagination—the poetic license, perhaps, of a religious ideologue—or of some kind of natural phenomenon that gave rise to the legend.

I was forcefully reminded of the Exodus tale when I first visited the town of Suez. The town was not out of bounds for military personnel, and if you got a pass and a ride, you could reach Suez in less than half an hour. The road leading to the town was, for the last mile or two, an elevated stone causeway with nothing but sand on either side, up to the town's first houses in the distance. Astonishingly, the second time I traveled this road, the causeway was totally surrounded by water on both sides. The Gulf of Suez ends in a shoal at its northern end, which is dry at low tide and immersed during surge. Could it be that this precise and awe-inspiring astronomical clockwork phenomenon was behind the Red Sea tale?

The task of Company 167 of the Royal Army Service Corps was to provide mobility and land transportation on the road along the Western bank of the canal, from Port Taufiq—the naval installation at Suez—up to Ismailiya in the north, half-way to Port Said, the canal's northern end. Keeping a large fleet of lorries in working condition was no trifling assignment, but thanks to cheap local labor—many of the hired hands arriving from Suez at dawn, incredibly, on foot—the job got done, and the enlisted men's role was converted to ruling over a hapless mass of bedraggled oil changers, tire inflators, and water adders.

The personnel of Company 167 were mostly British, but a few Jewish soldiers from Palestine were there when I arrived, and even Arab ones. Palestine, a British mandate, could not conscript, but was allowed to take volunteers, and for the Jewish community, joining the British army to fight against Germany was a matter of national priority. In view, however, of British policy prohibiting Jewish immigration to Palestine, one was trapped in this duality of allegiance. Ben-Gurion had famously defined the paradox, "We shall fight against the Germans as though there was no White Paper [curtailing immigration], and we shall fight against the British as though there was no war."

Leaving the canteen, an airless wet sauna during the NAAFI break, I am overwhelmed by the dry sauna outside, which evaporates body liquids swiftly and mercilessly much, perhaps, as a human soul evaporates from the body of a dying man. But there is something else in the air today: music, at full volume. Speakers, newly mounted on the illumination poles throughout the camp, are shrieking out a simple little tune, repeated endlessly. It is the national anthem of Egypt:

> King Farouk, King Farouk,
> Taa di daa di daa di daa,
> King Farouk, King Farouk,
> Taa di daa di daa di daa."

What is this? Are we celebrating Egypt's Independence Day?

Or is a local technician with a biting sense of humor 'testing' the new sound system? No. The anthem is played by authority. Trouble has developed in the civilian cinema at Suez, where at film's end the Egyptian anthem is played, and the populace stands to attention. Typically, servicemen in the audience ignore the occasion and walk out, often raucously. Unhappily, when questioned, the excuse given by the men was ignorance of the tune. Hence the free music lesson forced upon the camp.

The tug of war between soldiers and commanders has surely existed since armies were invented. In our tent one fellow, who planned to attend Cambridge after the war, helped the others appreciate the difference between officers and men. Men *sweat*, he instructed, while officers *perspire*. This was to be applied to a variety of other bodily functions, always with two appropriate and contrasting verbs. I must admit my English vocabulary, as well as my knowledge of anatomy, improved markedly.

One of the Arab soldiers at the workshops, a jolly fellow who said he was from Palestine, approached me for a small loan. Believing in maintaining friendly relations with our Arab neighbors, I loaned him a few pounds. Strangely, from that day on he was no longer seen around, perhaps taken ill or posted elsewhere. One Sunday afternoon I went looking for him, passing among tents where Arabic was spoken. Entering one tent, there he was, reclining on his cot, surrounded by a bunch of laughing buddies. A sudden silence fell on the group. The Arab comrade got up and declared loudly, "You are not my friend." Starting toward me, I thought this signaled trouble when, reaching me, he continued, "You are my *brudda*," and embraced me in front of all his friends. Was this a traditional *Sulha* ritual, a forgiveness ceremony, or an improvised performance of a sharp conniver? The debt was never mentioned again.

I was promoted to lance-corporal and became a motorcycle rider on the Suez-Ismailiya road. My job was to halt our company vehicles and inspect their transit papers, to make sure the trucks were not being deceptively misused. I liked the tropical architecture of the Suez Canal Company buildings along the road, airy wooden structures with broad verandas dating from the Canal's opening days in 1869. I also discovered that the higher the motorcycle's velocity, the cooler the temperature for the rider. I liked those hours on the road, away from the camp and the local labor.

When my turn came for a week's holiday, I chose a visit to Egypt's ancient monuments rather than a short home vacation, and I was astounded by what I saw. If the land of Goshen had given rise to an enduring primordial legend, even to the birth of a nation, the Nile valley had bequeathed to the world an extraordinary treasure of art and architecture, preceding the Goshen crossing by several thousand years, and withstanding the ravages of climate, earthquakes, wars, and pilferage as though time had stood still for five millennia. I saw the Luxor Temple, the Temple of Karnak, the Valley of the Kings, Abu Simbel, the Temple of Hatshepsut, the Great Sphinx, and the Pyramids of Giza, and took many photographs, in an era before mass publication of Egyptian antiquity books became the vogue. Staying in Luxor at the Old Winter Palace Hotel, opened in 1886 and now empty but for a small number of army personnel, it was particularly pleasant to watch the sun set across the Nile from the little garden near the hotel entrance. It was easy to forget there was a war on.

Back in Suez, I remember once, in the noon hours of a

particularly scorching day, a whispered rumor circulated through the camp: *there is water in the showers.* The message sounded unlikely, but surely deserved examination. One by one those in the know approached the shower-house and entered stealthily. Incredibly, the rumor was true—a veritable miracle of an unseen modern-day Moses. Instantly we were naked and under the sprays. In a flash the shower-house filled up, everyone screaming for joy, caution thrown to the winds.

Suddenly the sergeant-major was among us, shouting desperately to be heard. Enraged, he caught one of the naked fellows and addressed him as befits his rank and the occasion. It was my Arab *brudda* who was caught. Undaunted, the fellow raised his arms innocently and said apologetically, "Me no English." To everyone's disbelief, he turned away calmly and continued his douche. Absurdly, the audacious ploy worked. At once, none of us could fathom what the poor sergeant-major was trying to say, and like a wounded animal, humbled and seething, he stormed out.

No time to waste now. In an instant we were dressed and fleeing, hiding at a safe distance to observe further developments. Indeed, here came the sergeant-major again, gesticulating, the CO (Commanding Officer) and a bunch of other officers and interpreters in tow. Triumphantly they entered the shower-house, then reemerged, visibly baffled. They lingered for a while, and finally dispersed. Any trace of water on the hot shower floor had most certainly evaporated by the time they arrived.

Months passed. The tiny puppy dog raised furtively by the Cambridge fellow in our tent came of age, and one morning half the dog population of Suez was suddenly there, flying through the barbed wire unharmed like trained circus animals. For a full day and night the deafening, vicious orgy swept unpredictably throughout the camp, like the core of a tornado. In the end the young bitch ran off with the pack, probably to live happily ever after in the garbage-strewn alleys of Suez. It was a day to remember: May 8, 1945. Germany had surrendered. The war in Europe was over.

Less than three months later, Clement Attlee was elected Prime Minister of the United Kingdom, ousting Churchill. Sipping a Lamoun in the canteen that evening, I pondered the quirks of fate, as Chaucer had once put it, 'of him that stood in great prosperity and is y-fallen out of high degree in misery.' The canteen was almost empty. Gently I woke the Egyptian sleeping behind the counter, and bought a standard stamped air-letter form.

The next morning an orderly came to summon me to the CO. I knew, of course, what this would most likely be about, but did not share my hunch with the inquisitive messenger who accompanied me to the HQ tent.

It would be my second time in the CO's presence. The first time, soon after my arrival in Suez, I was on 'stick orderly' duty one night, hanging about HQ mainly to bring the CO a cup of tea from time to time. I had just brought a fresh cup from the canteen, when the sergeant-major, handling the change I had brought back, accidentally dropped a few coins into the CO's tea cup. For a moment, we shared a bit of a smile. I suggested I'd go and bring another cup, but the sergeant-major rejected that. With two fingers he started fishing the coins out of the milky brew. Judging by the man's black-rimmed fingernails, he must have been a mechanic some time in his earlier days. But when he had finally retrieved the coins, the rims of two of his fingernails were a perfect white. "Let me fetch another," I put forward again, but he said "No," and ordered me to carry the vile potion in to the CO.

This time as I entered, the sergeant-major stared at me as if I had completely lost my mind. Without a word, he motioned me to enter the Holy of Holies. I walked in and saluted, then remained at attention. The CO sat behind a simple wooden table, one that might have been ill-crafted in Suez, bare but for a letter-opener and a stamped air-letter next to it, light-blue. The address was handwritten, in my handwriting:

Sir Winston Churchill
10, Downing Street
London, England

"At ease," said the CO, and I complied smartly, staring at an eye level point in front of me, above the CO's head. After a pause, he lifted the air-letter and inquired, "Did you write this letter, lance-corporal?"

Never before did my rank sound so lowly. "Yes, Sir," I replied.

Patiently he explained that in the army, if you have a complaint, you don't write to the prime minister, you go to your corporal.

"Yes, Sir," I agreed.

"Do you have a complaint?"

"No, Sir."

There was a brief silence. Then he lifted the letter-opener.

"Do you mind if I open it?"

To this day I wonder what he would have done had I said, 'Yes Sir, I do mind, Sir. Letters ought to be opened by those to whom they are addressed.' But even if his question was a rhetorical one, or even if it was meant to be nasty, I could not but admire the sense of fairness he displayed. He waited for my response. For a moment I felt remorse for colluding with the sergeant-major in the tea episode long ago. Admittedly, I could not have disobeyed the sergeant-major then, but I could have conveniently stumbled, fallen flat on the ground, and spilt the loathsome liquid before reaching the CO. "No Sir, I do not mind," I said, as therein, I was almost certain, lay my exoneration.

Carefully he cut the letter open and read. In it, I expressed gratitude to Mr. Churchill for conducting and winning the war. I likened Sir Winston to the Biblical Moses, leading the Free World from tyranny to liberty, from bondage to freedom. And I noted sadly that like Moses himself, he was now barred from entering the Promised Land.

The CO took his time before he spoke. He'd received a request, he finally said, to send a suitable candidate to an instructors' course in the Army Education Corps. Would I be interested? I said I would, but that in truth my aspirations were eventually to seek a commission. If I go to the course and do well, he said, he'd recommend me to an officer selection board. With that, the interview was over. "Thank you, Sir," I said, saluted, and withdrew. On my way out, the sergeant-major followed me with a look of genuine pity.

The CO kept his word. I was sent to the course of the Army Education Corps, and following that to the Officer Selection Board at Mahdi, near Cairo, where I made the grade, the only one out of a group of eight. Waiting for my transfer to England, I was stationed at the huge old fortress-like building of the Heliopolis Transit Camp in Cairo. Here my 'fatigue' duty, twice daily, was to accompany and guard two prisoners, lifers I was told, on their short trek taking food from the kitchen across the parade ground back to the prisoners' wing. The old building, erected in the 1880's, contained some precious treasures too. A seemingly forgotten chapel with a real pipe organ became a haven for the rest of my days in Egypt. Never had J. S. Bach sounded so majestic, even without playing the foot keyboard, for which, I am certain, one needs two brains.

By troopship I traveled from Port Said, via British Cyprus and British Malta, to Toulon, and by military train through France, which lay in ruins, and across the Channel, to the Canterbury Transit Camp where I would wait for the start of the next officers' course. There, in the crowded NAAFI the night I arrived, I tried some long forgotten Mozart on the honky-tonk remnant of an upright. A soldier, short of build, came by and listened for a while. I remember him well, because he was the first person to speak to me in England, and he was clearly no stranger to music. "What is your instrument?" I asked. "I don't play," he said, but added shyly, "My father is a symphony conductor," and almost reluctantly, answering my question, "You may have heard of him, Thomas Beecham." I almost fell off the rickety piano chair. Much as I would have liked to see him again, I did not run into him anymore. Finally, I reported to the famous Officer Cadet Training Unit at Aldershot, and began my military education. I never saw Suez again.

Not long after the war, in a military coup, King Farouk, the British proxy, was deposed and forced to abdicate. Brashly, revolutionary Egypt nationalized the Suez Canal, and although it was twice wrenched from her in battle, Suez was twice returned. One by one, exotic crown jewels served by the Canal— Aden, Bahrain, Singapore, Hong Kong, not to mention India,

Nepal, Ceylon, the Maldives, Burma, Malaya, even Cyprus and Malta—dropped off the Empire tree like over-ripe fruit falling to the ground.

The British sun East of Suez had set. It rose no more.

King Farouk King Farouk

The view from my tent

The well-maintained vehicles of our transport company

Oil changers, tire inflators, and water adders

5

The Graduate

M.A. in Theater Arts, UCLA, 1951

After years of military service, it was finally time to think of pursuing an education. The place to go was, of course, the USA, the new leader of the world; and the first University I applied to, the University of California at Los Angeles, accepted me right away, giving me credit even for my music studies, in addition to my matriculation. Together with my cousin Kaly, who was headed to UC Berkeley to study engineering, we boarded a slow boat to the New World. Throwing anchor in places like Port Said, Piraeus, and Valetta, we were reminded of just how lucky we were to be on our way to a higher education. Youngsters half our age were swimming out to the ship and diving for coins that passengers were throwing into the water in their direction. Here and there kids were actually on board trying to sell trinkets, and speculation abounded that they had climbed up the anchor chains before daybreak.

I suppose most young people going abroad for a higher education know exactly what they intend to study, and what they would like to do later in life. This was not the case with me. Admittedly, I was attracted to the arts, but my upbringing was too conventional to risk a Bohemian life. Besides, I realized I was clearly not good enough to become, say, a professional pianist. Engineering did not fascinate me, and in mathematics I was lousy. I did not really know what I should be doing. Luckily, I was not asked this question before, not even upon admission to the university, and so I was able to delay the choice all the way to America. But eventually, here I was at UCLA registration, required to list my courses.

Leafing through the catalogue for the umpteenth time, I felt a raised heartbeat every time I came across the page with the newly established 'Motion Picture Division of the Theater Arts Department.' Here, it seemed, the curriculum contained all I could ever wish for–literature, history, drama, theater, photography, even music. One lives only once, went through my head, and I filled the list without hesitation.

The new film school at UCLA was housed behind Royce Hall, the campus' main edifice, in a temporary wooden structure, painted green, which contained a small sound stage, a few editing rooms, camera and sound recording equipment, and two offices, one occupied by the film school's young head Norman Dyhrenfurth, and the other, perhaps to add prestige to the new venture, by the chairman of the Theater Arts Department, the much respected stage and screen producer Kenneth Macgowan. Film was seen in the department as an outgrowth of theater, and the program included a strong background in drama. I threw myself into this discipline with all the passion and determination I was capable of. Dyhrenfurth, a self-assured and affable Swiss documentary film-maker and an enthusiastic mountain climber, taught us not only the intricacies of film equipment and technique, but also the importance of teamwork. In deference, no doubt, to his mountain-climbing passion, he once took us to the California snow-covered mountains to practice camera workshop, and to work and live together as a team.

The first person I met in Los Angeles was Irving Weschler. He arrived at the Jewish Fraternity House on the same morning as I and, assigned to sharing a room, we quickly became friends. He had come from NY to study for his doctorate in Labor Relations. But what drew us together was our mutual European background. He and his parents were originally from Vienna, they had arrived in the US at the last minute, after the *Anschluss*, and his mother was a well known piano teacher. Soon Irv and I decided to move out of the fraternity and rent a small apartment. We needed a third partner, and selected a foreign student from Greece named Aristides Anagnostopolous, a choice that proved to be most agreeable. Aris Anagnos, as he was later known, eventually remained in the USA, became a hugely successful real estate magnate, and a dedicated activist and donor to world-wide issues of social justice.

Irv started dating a girl named Franzi Toch, the daughter of the Austrian expatriate composer Ernst Toch. The first time Franzi invited Irv to her parents' house, she invited the three of us, known in the Toch household as *Das Dreibueberlhaus* (House of the Three Boys), modeled on the popular operetta with Schubert's music *Das Dreimaederllhaus* (House of the Three Girls). A practical joker, Franzi did not tell her parents, when we arrived, which one of us was her boyfriend. Many years later Franzi's mother, on a visit to Israel, told me that she and her husband were divided on this issue. She had thought that Franzi's choice was Aristides, while Toch thought it was I. Nonetheless Franzi's romance with Irv led to a wedding, the ceremony taking place in the Toch garden of their comfortable house in Santa Monica, where Toch's composition *Dedication*, written in the young couple's honor, was premiered by the renowned Budapest String Quartet. Decades later in Israel, I performed the rare piece, written in late Romantic style, with the strings of a full orchestra, and the effect was impressive and luscious.

Among the small band of film students were two brothers, Dennis and Terry Sanders, who invited me to come one evening to their home in Los Angeles, way up one of the Canyon Drives. I found the address, a fine two-storey building at the top of a hill. But the place was dark and empty, and it turned out to be but the gate-house. On exploring the grounds, I found the main building, and when no one answered my ring, I opened the door and walked in. A long corridor led to an immense living room, well lit, in the middle of which stood a motionless naked woman, while a large group was sketching her in complete silence. The boys' mother, a wealthy dowager, as I soon learnt, had brought a number of survivors from the Holocaust to the USA, and had married one of them. Sadly, her new husband had fallen ill and was bed ridden, hence every day of the week there was some cultural activity in the house in which he could participate. Dennis and Terry, both modest and unassuming, took their film studies seriously. They shot a short film titled *Time Out Of War*, which won an Academy Award for Best Short Subject, 1955.

During my stay in Los Angeles I widened my education not only in class. Irv and Franzi remained my closest friends, and at the Toch house on Friday nights I met some of the most famous German and Austrian expatriates. One evening there was a reading at the home of Lion Feuchtwanger of his *Jephta and his Daughter,* which he was writing then, in German. The English translation of the first chapter was read by Norman Corwin, the writer, who had a marvelous voice. I was intrigued to discover in a small cubicle off the living room an organ, perhaps a chamber organ, the first time I had seen such an instrument in a home. I also remember the first time I entered the home of the aging Arnold Schoenberg. His young son, then aged four or five, came rolling down the stairs from the upper floor neatly packed inside an inflated rubber tube, and immensely proud of having scared me to death. At the Tochs, I met the famous Alma Mahler Werfel, then in her eighties and heavy of movement, but her face was smooth as a baby's and her light blue eyes sparkled. "I will give you one of Werfel's books," she said to me, "and you film it." This was, of course, way out of my reach, but I was deeply flattered. Age, it seemed, did not change dear Alma. She continued to do what she had done so well in years gone by—inspire extraordinary artistic creation.

Irv and Franzi had four children in quick succession, two of them, Lawrence and Toni Weschler, grew up to become successful authors. But tragedy hit the family, twice: Irv was killed in an automobile accident while still in his thirties, and Franzi, more than twenty years later, also died when run over by a car.

At UCLA I met a young Israeli pianist who played a concert at Royce Hall. His name was Menahem Pressler, and he was on his way to Mills College in Oakland, where he was to study with the well-known pianist and teacher Egon Petri. Pressler went on to become one of the most prominent musicians of our time; he was the founder and pianist of the *Beaux Arts Trio,* and to this day is Distinguished Professor of Music at Indiana University. It was between semesters when he came through, and we decided to drive up together to San Francisco in my jalopy. We went via U.S. Highway 1, and enjoyed one of the most breathtaking journeys along the winding road overlooking the Pacific. Petri welcomed his new student and me, and told us the story of how in his childhood it was decided that he should become a pianist. "Liszt told my parents I should take up the violin, like my father, who was a professional violinist, but Brahms said I should learn the piano."

Once I was invited to a party where suddenly the hostess announced to the assembly, "I want you to meet two guests tonight, the sister of King Farouk from Egypt, and a student at UCLA from Israel." Unaware of this furtively planned confrontation, I said, "Oh Princess, I spent two years in your ancient country, in the British Army during the war." The Princess graciously replied, "And I have been in your country many times. I bought all my fur coats in Tel-Aviv."

My years in California passed intensively, both at the University, where I earned a B.A. and an M.A. in Theater Arts, and afterwards gained invaluable experience in the field, both in the documentary realm, such as filming a medical mission in the Sudan, and in studio work, such as being second unit director for Mervyn LeRoy in Hawaii. Returning home with a feeling of accomplishment, I nevertheless felt a sense of unfinished business, which I concluded only thirty years later, when I got a PhD in Theater Arts at Tel-Aviv University, in 1980.

Although at UCLA we were required to read many plays, I was astonished at the dearth of theoretical background concerning dramatic literature. In music there are several well defined forms, such as the Variations form or the famous Sonata form, which details the advance of a musical composition in terms of structure and harmony. The sonata form theory actually developed hand in hand with the naissance of sonata form music itself, as epitomized in the works of several of Bach's sons and mainly by Haydn, Mozart, and Beethoven.

Here, by contrast, was a continuous wealth of drama, some of it two and a half thousand years old, and beyond Aristotle's *Poetics,* with very little theory to guide us. This shortage preoccupied me throughout the years. If music had detailed rules for analysis and composition, why did not literature?

I received a strong impetus to look for a better understanding in these matters from none other than Artur Rodzinski, the famous conductor and a devoted follower of film and drama. I had met the Rodzinskis in Rome where they lived in the late '50s, when I was there working on Fred Zinnemann's *The Nun's Story.* "Where is the drama in the Nun's Story?" Rodzinski demanded of me. He had read Kathryn Hulme's book, and indeed playwright Robert Anderson's screenplay, which he had not read, did not diverge much from its source. Rodzinski could not have scored a better point, as this was precisely the question I was asking myself. In the story, the daughter of a Belgian surgeon decides to become a nun, is sent to Africa to serve in a remote jungle hospital, and eventually decides to leave the religious life. Is this really the stuff of drama?

I had no reply for Rodzinski then and when, years later, I thought I had found the answer, Rodzinski had died. The most essential and obligatory elements in a dramatic story, I reasoned, were *Leading Character* and *Conflict*, the latter comprised of two opposing forces, at least one of which is embedded in the leading character. *The Nun's Story*, I came to realize, followed a pattern that could be found in other literary works, indicating perhaps that it belonged to a specific archetype, or class, of story: **A leading character advances a certain force consistently, but in the end, quite abruptly, chooses to abandon it.** This would fit not only the *Nun's Story*, but also Ibsen's *A Doll's House*, and Sophocles' *Antigone.* Only the leading character and the conflict differ from play to play, but the essence and the structure of the story remain the same.

This led me to seek other archetypes of stories, and I soon discerned one closely related: **A leading character advances a certain force consistently, without ever abandoning it, sometimes even at the cost of his life.** Examples of this are Robert Bolt's play *A Man for All Seasons*, which also became a very successful Fred Zinnemann film, and the Bible's Book of Job. Here the leading character is going through a series of tribulations, with mounting intensity, vaguely reminiscent of the Variations form in music, but in contrast to the previous archetype, he sticks to his position without wavering to the very end.

In time I discovered a limited number of additional archetypes of stories. The one I found most exciting was when both forces of the conflict gain entry into the protagonist's soul: **A leading character is torn within his soul between two opposing forces, and in the end chooses both, one after the other, in a preordained order.** For my doctorate I picked six famous plays belonging, in my view, to this group, and followed their advance step by step. The plays were Sophocles' *Oedipus* (425 B.C.), Shakespeare's *Hamlet* (1601) and *Othello* (1605), Pirandello's *Henry IV* (1929), Brecht's *Galileo* (1938), and H.E.Bates' and David Lean's romantic screen comedy *Summer Madness* (1956), based on Arthur Laurents' stage play *The Time of the Cuckoo* (1952).

Much as these works are dissimilar in any of the established traditional criteria, they do have the above feature in common. Thus Othello, torn between his love for Desdemona and his jealousy of her, strangles Desdemona, but overcome by the knowledge of her innocence and his love for her, he stabs himself to death. Similarly, American spinster Jane Hudson (Katherine Hepburn) of *Summer Madness,* on a holiday in Venice, is torn between emotional restraint and emotional involvement. Toward the end, she embarks on a future-less affair with a married Italian man, but changes her mind and goes home to Ohio alone. Tragedy or Comedy, both stories belong in the same category.

Looking at the plays in closer range, I made what seemed to me the most astonishing observation. All six works follow a similar advance of their stories in fairly minute detail, passing through close to forty stations, or steps (thirty nine, to be exact), almost without exception. This suggests the existence of a hitherto unnoticed structural blueprint the poets follow, even if consciously perhaps unaware of its being. In 2004 my hypothesis was published in the USA in a small volume titled *The 39 Steps of Self-Division.* Only then did I feel that my education at UCLA had finally been completed.

Film workshop: "Camera!...

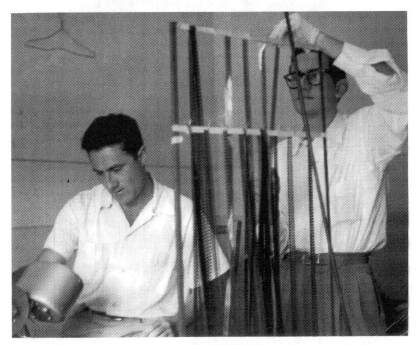

"...Cut!"

6

Making Uirapuru

Our entire production crew

In 1950 the Theater Arts department at UCLA was one of only two or three universities in the world where film-making was being taught. While looking for a theme for my MA thesis, I happened one day into a neighborhood music store, and was attracted by a striking LP record cover. It was a recording, just released, of Heitor Villa-Lobos' symphonic tone poem *Uirapuru*, a novel, intricate work, written in 1917, describing an Indian-Brazilian legend of love, transformation, and loss. The powerful, exotic music, evocative of a Diaghilev ballet, as well as the legend itself, moved me to envisage a film to fit the music, in which the legend would be acted out in pantomime by authentic Indians in the Brazilian jungle.

'Uirapuru' is the name of a small singing bird, perching high in the trees of the rain forest, believed to have magical powers in bringing love to whoever captures or kills it. A beautiful Indian maiden, so the legend goes, manages to pierce an Uirapuru with her bow and arrow, and as the little bird falls to the ground, it transforms into a handsome young man. There is great joy among the tribesmen as the maiden guides her newfound love back toward her jungle clearing. But soon an ugly old Indian, the evil spirit of the forest, boldly confronts the young couple, and with his bow and arrow shoots the young man through the heart. As he dies, the handsome young Indian changes back into an Uirapuru, which flies away, leaving the maiden alone and grief-stricken.

Luckily, the Theater Arts department, chaired by Professor Kenneth MacGowan, accepted my request to submit a film instead of a written MA paper, the usual academic procedure until then. It was primarily the athletic-looking head of the department's film division, Norman Dyhrenfurth, who supported my plea to allow students to actually make student films for credit. Luckily also, Villa-Lobos, who lived in Rio de Janeiro, granted me permission to use his composition for the film. The New York Philharmonic, which had recorded the piece with Efrem Kurtz conducting, allowed its use for the sound track. And a young consul at the Brazilian embassy in Los Angeles, Vinicius de Moraes, arranged a flight for me on an empty Brazilian Air Force plane, with overnight stops in Trinidad and Paramaribo, to Belem do Para, a sleepy little town at that time, on the mouth of the Amazon River.

It is significant to note that in the years to come, Professor Dyhrenfurth, a dedicated second-generation mountain-climber, headed the famed American Himalaya Expedition of 1963, and became the first American to conquer Mt. Everest, an achievement for which he was honored in the White House by President Kennedy. Vinicius de Moraes, the diplomat turned poet, went on to become one of Brazil's most celebrated lyricists, whose popular play *Orfeu do Carnaval* became, in 1959, the Academy-Award-winning film *Orfeo Negro*. Were it not for the support of these two extraordinary men, I would never have landed so far from the university or, for that matter, from my home country, Israel.

Belem, its name distorted from the word *Bethlehem*, became my base camp. Here I would determine the most suitable tribe for our purpose, prepare the expedition in detail, and collect the provisions to be taken along. My mentor in all this was the area manager of the government's 'Service for the Protection of Indians,' Senhor Miranda. Middle-aged, heavy-set, perspiring and short of breath, he was forever dressed in pajamas, which seemed paradoxically to elevate his status. Twice a year he would visit distant outposts of the *Servicio*, bringing with him whatever meager medical supplies and scant humanitarian aid he could muster for the quickly vanishing Indian population.

My billet for those few weeks in Belem was the Hotel Garez, a crumbling old residence converted into a small pension. Madame Garez, the domineering owner, could be heard all day shouting instructions in broken French to her frightened, docile staff. Quiet during the day, at night the Garez sprang to life. A local band played in the garden below my window, and sleep before the early hours of the morning was out of the question. Lying awake listening, the slow songs of longing, juxtaposed against the syncopated Latin rhythms, such as *Desde Ontem* (*Only Yesterday* in free translation)*,* or *Triste es el alma* (*Sad is the Soul*)*,* captivated me. I began to watch the pianist from close range, and when the fellow invited me to play instead of him, I discovered a new and exciting brand of chamber music. This became routine, the pianist being pleased to have some time off. To my surprise, the harsh Madame Garez, upon my departure, gave me a generous discount on my bill for my services in her nightclub.

Joining me in Belem, intrigued by the project, was Peter Paul Hilbert, a recently arrived German ex-army officer employed as an anthropologist at the local *Goeldi* Museum. We had met at the luxurious tropical villa of the American consul in Belem, the elderly and much-respected US diplomat George Coleman, who suggested that Peter, having explored Indian tribes in the interior, could be of valuable assistance if he were to join me. Indeed, I liked Peter from the start, in addition to realizing the vital contribution he could make. At the same time I felt an unsettling discomfort, considering our disparate national backgrounds and the shattering events of recent history. My misgivings were alleviated when Peter adamantly declined Senhor Miranda's insistence that we take firearms with us for self-protection. Peter's view of entering and facing the Indians unarmed validated my trust in him. He took a two-month leave of absence from the *Goeldi* to come with me.

At the *Goeldi,* Peter illustrated to me some of the rain forest features. In one aquarium were kept the much-dreaded tiny piranhas, actually quite harmless-looking silvery little fish, swimming about peacefully. On a string Peter lowered a piece of raw meat into the water, and in a split second the piranhas homed in wildly on the snack and backed out again, leaving Peter with an empty string. Piranhas attack only when activated by blood, but a minor scratch is enough to turn an injured party into a skeleton.

Before venturing into the rain forest, I paid a courtesy visit to an aging, chain-smoking Villa-Lobos in Rio, who received me warmly, first in his large yet ramshackle office at the Ministry of Education, empty but for a tiny picture of J. S. Bach hanging on the wall behind him, and later at his small yet cozy apartment, his attentive wife Arminda at his side. Villa-Lobos suggested that I look up his good friend, the octogenarian General Candido Rondon in Sao Paulo, founder and director of the Service for the Protection of Indians. The legendary general, who had earned his fame in the 1890s for laying the first telegraph lines through the Brazilian jungles, provided me with much useful information and a fascinating, illustrated volume of Indian culture authored by him. It was this diminutive visionary, allegedly part-Indian, who in 1916 had invited Villa-Lobos to join him on one of his expeditions to the interior, a trip which provided the composer with the inspiration to create the work. Inexplicably, the piece was never performed for almost 20 years, and was first recorded only weeks before I heard it in that neighborhood music shop in Los Angeles.

Armed with a 16mm Bolex camera and a limited supply of Kodak color film, Peter and I embarked on the rather dubious adventure, first to *find* Indians, who were rapidly retreating deeper and deeper into the woods, and then to persuade them to *act out* the legend for the camera. It was decided that we would make our way up the Gurupi river, south of and parallel to the Amazon, as the Amazon itself would have no Indians left until beyond Manaos, over two thousand kilometers up the gigantic waterway. The tribe recommended to us was the Urubu, known for their beautiful feather-wear and, perhaps to relieve any apprehensions I might have harbored, reputed to be a peaceful lot, having killed relatively few whites. We thus traveled by narrow rail along the Atlantic coast to Braganca, a forgotten little town at the mouth of the Gurupi, and up the river in a rickety supply vessel to Viseu, a tiny solitary village populated by one Lebanese family, the Rashids, who spoke Arabic among themselves. We had reached civilization's end station. There was nothing beyond this point but jungle.

By Senhor Miranda's prior arrangement, the Rashids' prized outboard motor was made available to us, and next morning we were all set to embark on our way to the *Servicio's* remote outpost deep within Indian territory. We waved goodbye to a friendly gathering near the water, Viseu's entire population. The antiquated outboard, however, failed to start, and after countless attempts the motor had to be carried up the river bank, dismantled under a shady tree, and reassembled again. The next try did not fare better, and the procedure repeated itself for days, an eager group of spectators, mostly children, following the steadfast Rashid brothers up and down the hill, each time, for certain, key engine-parts spread about being lost in the sand. By week's end, and by some uncanny miracle, the motor sprang to life.

Peter and I and a few itinerant porters finally set out. The small boat was heavy, carrying our sundry equipment, provisions, food supplies, medical aid, and also salt, beads, and cloth for the Indians. Not forgotten was a full barrel of gasoline for the outboard, placed, for balance and for safety, at the boat's bow. Thus we journeyed into nature's no-man's-land, treacherous, muddy, piranha-infested waters surrounding us and stretching out ahead. Both sides of the river were flanked by thick, monotonous mangrove trees, positioned on tangled roots in the water, rather than on land. Occasionally some animal roared, frightened by the engine's clatter, or perhaps excitedly protesting man's ruthless, uninvited incursion.

A few days later, the malfunctioning engine caught fire and the boat went up in flames. By sheer luck we extinguished the blaze before it reached the fuel barrel. Floating helplessly downstream, we managed to requisition an old dugout canoe, and continued our thrust upstream. Gone, however, was the luxury cruise; from now on we had to make do with hand paddles. One seat wide, the canoe's balance was precarious, there was no leg room, and very quickly painful blisters formed on the palms of our hands. Despite our hard work, we barely made progress. Where the river tapered and the current became stronger, we would actually lose ground, and when we encountered *cachueras*, small rapids, we were on the brink of disaster, saved only by our boatmen's cunning navigation and graceful pirouetting. Nights we would select a landing, cut the bush, and hang our hammocks. One morning, stepping out of my hammock, the ground under my foot started to move, and to my dismay I saw that I had stepped on the back of a crocodile. The beast, seemingly disinterested in me, gently vacated its resting place under my hammock, and slid noiselessly into the water. For several weeks we traveled this way, depleting our rations too soon, and at times wondering whether we would ever reach our destination.

Peter was nine years my senior, and quite musical. In his native Berlin before the war, he had sung in a choir, and once performed under the great Wilhelm Furtwaengler. On the brown, inhospitable waters we sang rounds, German ones I remembered from my childhood in Europe, and Hebrew ones I taught him. It had been his unrelenting refusal to join the Nazi party that enabled him to emigrate after the war. The toll he paid for being German, though, was high. He had spent six years in the army, his studies were interrupted and incomplete, his leg had been severely mangled in Russia, and his aging father, hastily inducted days before the war ended to defend crumbling Berlin, was immediately killed.

We reached the outpost finally. Senhor Miranda had postulated that we stay there, the *servicio* man on duty having been notified to accommodate us. The plan was to do the film right there, the outpost being the central gathering point for all Indian tribes in the area. Alas, we found the station all but abandoned. The Indians, we were told, had moved away or died, most likely of the common cold, a white man's disease for which the Indians possessed no natural immunity. Peter, I think, suspected the anthropologist's inescapable truth. To find Indians, a white man must abandon the water and trek through the woods on foot.

Following a few half-Indians who offered to guide us, we carried our packs and pushed through the bush, single file. The blocked-out sun, eclipsed by the enormous trees, and the dense undergrowth, completely deactivated one's sense of direction. So thick was the growth that it took but a few steps' distance for the guide ahead to become obscured and vanish. At times the guides became anxious, freezing in their track, smelling a wild animal nearby; or they would suddenly race furiously, lifting their feet in frenzy, escaping from a nest of giant, poisonous fire ants. Peter and I withstood the exhausting trek pretty well, and we credited our resilience to the officers' training we both had, he in the Wehrmacht and I in the Haganah and in the British Army.

Peter told me of the difficulty anthropologists experienced when trying to enter Indian territory. Suspicious of the white man, often with good reason, many well intentioned visitors were met with violence and death. One well-known ethnologist who had been successful in breaking into a particularly hostile tribe was German born Kurt Unckel, later known as Curt Nimuendaju (1883–1945). Approaching the Indians, he threw all his gear and clothing into the river, and met his hosts dressed the way he was born. His daring stratagem worked. No ill befell him thus.

The small band of stone-age Urubu Indians we finally encountered seemed as astonished to see us as we were to discover them. The men wore nothing but a few feathers of radiant colors around their forearms and ankles, a large feather hanging out of their pierced lower lip. Some, their bodies painted with stripes of black and red, wore necklaces of animal-teeth, and most were armed with bow and arrow. This was a hunting party, one of our porters conversant in Tupi-Guarani, enlightened us. The group belonged to the jungle clearing of Chieftain Piahu where, it was soon agreed, we would be guided, and where eventually, upon presenting the chief with the cloth and the other gifts we had brought with us, we were accepted peacefully and offered shelter in a small vacant grass hut.

Luck was on our side. Quickly we were able to cast our Maiden and her Man, as well as the evil old Indian. There were, however, altogether too few Indians to provide the proper scope for the film, particularly for staging the score's wild, primeval dance celebrating the young man's coming to life. Word of our arrival must have spread far and wide through the jungle, for in a day or two masses of Indians materialized in our clearing. They won't stay long, Peter warned me, and we hastily shot the big dance scene right away, after which the many visitors did indeed disperse, disappearing into the jungle as quietly as they had come.

The Indians were of course innocent of our purpose and our doings. Nevertheless, they obligingly cooperated with our seemingly bizarre requests. At first I tried to communicate through an interpreter, actually via two. I would articulate the desired action to Peter in German, Peter would describe it to our porter in Portuguese, and the porter would convey it to the tribesmen in Tupi-Guarani. If an Indian had a question, the message would be relayed back to me in reverse. Soon, however, long discourses between the porter and the Indian would ensue, which neither Peter nor I understood. In his eagerness to restore order, Peter would sometimes inadvertently address me in Portuguese, and the poor porter in German. Clearly, this did not get us very far. Instead, before each shot, I would perform the action myself, run behind the camera and shoot, while the actors imitated me in good humor and without inhibition. Two words I quickly learnt in Tupi met my directorial needs: good ('*katu*'), and once more ('*amu*'). In the absence of dialogue in the film, there was no need for a regular screenplay. The orchestral score was the basis for the film, and a carefully planned story board saw to it that all the music was covered by appropriate visual images.

Peter did not cease to amaze me. Every morning he tended to the sick, mostly those with simpler cuts or bruises. We had been warned not to tend to the seriously ill, as that might endanger our lives in the event the patient should die, and in some cases we sadly heeded this admonition. Another remarkable quality was Peter's unyielding habit of shaving every day, an inconvenience I gladly relinquished in favor of growing a beard. Throughout our stay Peter made copious notes and sketches of plants and utensils. One Indian seemed particularly fascinated by the drawing process, and when Peter offered him pencil and paper, he laboriously drew a short zigzagged line on the empty page. Pleased, apparently, with his creation, the Indian proudly returned the page to Peter. What is it, Peter asked, intrigued. A crocodile, the man answered.

I had brought a stuffed Uirapuru with me, and a smoke canister for the transformation scene, in which the young man would step out from a cloud of smoke. The stuffed bird came in handy, but the canister, once opened, instantly released its meager contents, leaving us in the lurch. The Indians quickly came to our rescue, bringing a climbing plant which upon burning produced thick smoke worthy of a modern battlefield.

As we worked, several young Indians became our regular crew. I had brought large rolls of tin foil with me to make reflectors, and, astonishingly, the crew became so adept at using them, especially for close-ups, that calling out lighting instructions quickly became superfluous.

Two tricky scenes to achieve were the young man's death and his re-transformation to bird. For his being shot, we bound a very thin wire, which I had brought along, around the young man's chest, one end extending outward from the area of his heart. Over the wire we attached a loosely moving tail end of an arrow, and sent it sliding down on the invisible wire to its target. In the finished film the shot became credible, particularly as it was preceded by a close shot of a metal arrowhead pulled backward into frame before its release, and was followed by a shot of the young man's collapse, tinged with an amount of Heinz Tomato Sauce I had included in our gear. The re-transformation scene was achieved later in the lab, a rising column of smoke printed backwards, showing the shrinking smoke reaching its source—the magic bird nestled in the maiden's hand.

Beyond the film's task of following the legend, the intent was to present the Indians' unadulterated way of life as genuinely as possible. We thus shot a variety of the tribe's daily activities, scenes that would be cut into the film to enhance its authenticity. One of these shots caused particular delight and bafflement among audiences: a young woman happily feeding a baby on one breast, and a small puppy dog on the other.

The film's ending, in which the grief-stricken maiden is left alone after the little bird had flown away, called for a gentle touch. There was of course no way of explaining the scene to our maiden nor of expecting her to express anguish. So we shot her as best we could, just crouching there. The result was surprising. Viewed in the finished film, the maiden appeared to show genuine grief, restrained by a dignified acceptance of her fate. Such is the power of a close-up in film-making.

Life in the clearing of Piahu was actually very pleasant. We built a table and a bench in our hut, something the Indians had never seen, hammocks being their only home furnishings. Prized were our discarded food cans, which could be used for making metal heads for their long arrows. My famous finger trick, by which I feigned to tear off part of my thumb, came in handy, and was a constant cause of wonderment, especially among the young, one of whom, sneaking behind my back, eventually uncovered my ruse.

Occasionally Peter and I indulged in a luxury we called milkshake, remnants of our milk and chocolate powders mixed with fresh water from the rivulet nearby. Our food supply, however, did not last long, and we soon had to switch to our hosts' hunter-gatherer fare, nibbling at unfamiliar and tasteless plants, and occasionally tearing off with our fingers and ingesting pieces from a roasted tortoise, placed live upside down into a fire.

Making a fire, incidentally, was by no means a simple feat for the tribesmen. It was achieved by patiently and laboriously rotating a thin stick of wood back and forth in the palms of one's hands, the stick being nestled in a bundle of dried moss which, when sufficiently heated, would begin to ignite. Most impressive were the tribe's geometrically decorated gourds, their artful feather combinations, the finely crafted combs used widely in caring for their long black hair, and their majestic ornamental headgear. Remarkable also were the rhythmic and melodic songs which, although sung only in unison, were to my total amazement all in perfect pentatonic scale. Could it have been adapted from the overtones left ringing faintly in the bow after an arrow had been released?

What the Indians did not have was a count of time or a sense of seasons, there being none in that latitude and climate. For me it was this lack of hours and years, more than anything else, which defined the twenty-thousand-year gulf between us. When the time came for us to leave, many of the tribesmen accompanied us for days until we reached the river, to say goodbye. Rarely in my life have I felt so honored.

Cut off from civilization for several months, we finally resurfaced in Viseu, thin and bedraggled, unsure of the day's date, but jubilant, with a pack of exposed though yet undeveloped film. Back in Belem we paid visits to Senhor Miranda, to Madame Garez, and to George Coleman. In the end, Peter saw me off to the airport. Our parting was sad, despite our vowing to stay in touch.

Peter eventually went back to Germany. He completed his doctorate and became an eminent Professor of Archeology, often digging in South America and researching at the Smithsonian Institute in Washington DC. We did stay in touch throughout the years, recurrently meeting in Europe and in Israel. Peter's older son Klaus (who became a famous archeologist himself), spent one summer during his gap year as a volunteer in Israel, picking apples on a kibbutz near the Lebanese border. Peter remained one of my closest friends until his death in 1989.

Returning to LA, I finished the film, which I simply titled *Uirapuru*. In cutting film to music, I discovered it was important to 'cut' (change from one shot to the next) exactly on the bar-line. Even more effective was having the action fit the music within a given shot. This would be easy to accomplish with the aid of a playback, but in the absence of such luxury I had to direct the action based on guessing the music's tempo on the record. One feature I adopted was a fast sequence of close-ups toward the end of the big dance scene, where shots followed each other so as to fit in with the beat. Never having seen such fast cutting, I feared this might fail, but the cumulative effect proved to be powerful. A frame to the whole story was provided by a starting shot of treetops panning down to reveal the tribe's clearing, and an ending shot of the grieving girl panning up to the very treetops we saw at the beginning. A fellow art student, Marvin Rubin, drew the titles, and UCLA Professor Walter Kingson, of radio fame, willingly recorded the short opening narration I had written.

I got my MA finally, with distinction. The film was shown several times at UCLA, where it attracted attention from leading figures in the industry, and it ran at New York's Cinema 16, where it won a prize. It was shown at the British Film Institute in London, at the Edinburgh Film Festival, at the Venice Bienale, and at a composers' conference in Paris, where Villa-Lobos himself presented it.

Thirty years later, at the First International Student Film Festival initiated and held at Tel-Aviv University, *Uirapuru* was shown as the first accredited student MA film. And fifty years later, in 2000, in my capacity as music director of the Campus Orchestra, I conducted Villa-Lobos' work, to warm public acclaim. It was *Uirapuru*'s first performance in Israel, and to my knowledge the only one to date.

Triste es el alma

Young mother with baby.
Note ornamented comb, humming-bird feathers on forehead and
cheeks, earrings, necklace, and body paint.

Urubu Song

The young man playing the legendary youth in the film

Warriors in the dance scene

Man wearing necklace of animal
teeth, feather in lower lip

Ornamented warrior

Pensive girl

Happy young woman
with comb

*With Peter, preparing the day's work
on the 'veranda' of our grass hut*

With two friends before departure

7

Trouble In Tahiti

An atoll in the Tuamotus

"The Pacific is inconstant and uncertain like the
soul of man," wrote Somerset Maugham.

The year was 1952. It was nearly two weeks that we had
seen no land. In silence we glided over the huge planet, hardly
recognizing it as our earth. The first few days were foggy and
overcast, but on the fourth day the sun came out and painted the
water deep blue, thrusting here and there, through the glossy

surface of the ocean, bottomless shafts of clear transparent light. Day after day we could watch the shadows at noon grow shorter, until they turned about and pointed northward. We were well into the Southern hemisphere, but beyond that we knew no more. All around us the water seemed to be one big mass of solid desert. It was quiet, and the ocean could not have a name more fitting.

The S.S. *Waihemo* ('Bitter Water' in Maori), under Captain White, had sailed from Los Angeles harbor one August afternoon on its regular Pacific run. It was a somewhat pitiful departure. No more than a handful of bystanders had waved the ship farewell, as the rusty freighter, loaded to the brim, began to gain distance from the dock. Lumber from Canada was piled high on the open decks. I stumbled over sacks of raw onions destined for Fiji, and caught my ankles between gas cylinders for the Cook Islands. Everywhere one was likely to lean up against wet paint. Nor was it actually that quiet on board. All day long the stubborn whine of electric hammers removing rust from the plates, like a dentist boring into a patient's tooth, sent cold shivers up my spine. And toward evening, when the work was done and the promise of a magnificent sunset was near, a shipment of breeding hens for New Caledonia exhausted themselves in loud and pointless revolt.

I placed a deck chair comfortably in the breeze and started to get acquainted with the Pacific. Quickly I discovered an amazing wealth of history, literature, and art. Herman Melville, Jack London, Somerset Maugham, had traveled extensively through the islands and their works written there rank among their best. Robert Louis Stevenson made his home in Samoa at the age of thirty two, and lived there until his death, alas only eight years later. The lush images of Paul Gaugin's Tahitian women were embedded in the West's collective consciousness. Charles Nordhoff and James Norman Hall, the late patriarchs of South Seas literature (*Mutiny on the Bounty*), went to Tahiti after World War 1 and never returned. Frederic O'Brien caused a mass movement of escapists to the islands. Beatrice Grimshaw captured the beauty of the Pacific. William Stone caught the innocence of Polynesia. Robert Dean Frisbie married a Polynesian girl and had five children with her, one of whom, a daughter, became a writer. Tom Neal spent a good part of his life alone on a small atoll, and lived to write about it. And since WW2, James Michener had emerged as the modern exponent of the South Pacific.

There were five other passengers besides me on board, and seven times a day we descended to the tiny saloon for meals, where early morning tea, breakfast, morning tea, lunch, afternoon tea, tea, and evening tea were served. Captain White, a stout, graying Australian and the only man on board wearing a uniform, presided. Eager to engage in conversation, he was a bit of a philosopher. "As you grow older," he once told us, "you like to be occupied. Long weekends lose their thrill. Idleness is a quality of youth."

Two of the passengers were young men from Utah on their way to a Mormon mission. One was a skinny farmhand barely twenty, the other a former barber, only a bit older. Much of the time they kept to themselves, studying their future duties. Neither had acquired special training for their new assignment. All they knew was that their mission would last two years, that they had to support themselves during their service, and that one did not refuse the church when invited to serve. Perhaps this lay approach, and the disciples' youthfulness, characteristic among the Mormon missionaries, could explain their great popularity in Polynesia. The Mormons could boast of the most active church in the islands, and their white modern temple in Papeete was "the only place in Oceania with a pipe organ and nine toilets."

Another passenger was Papa Michel, an aging, ill-tempered fellow, displaying two disfigured fingers when he spoke. Born on the islands–his father an American Navy captain, his mother a native Marquesan–Michel's home was nominally in Tahiti, where he lived, in his own words, "Christ, on the bum." A restless man, he often escaped to sea. He was a sailor long before the Panama Canal opened (1914), and he fought in Haiti in the US occupation of 1915. During WW1 he saw action in the Navy, for which he was decorated twice, and in WW2, while in the Merchant Marine, he fought in the Philippines. Michel was married to a Marquesan woman, and they had a grown daughter. "Those natives," he said suddenly and unexpectedly, "Christ, I can't stand them." But neither did Michel settle anywhere else. Every time the sea became too big, he returned home. This time he was coming home for good, too old even for the small ferry in Morocco, his last job. "If only we could arrive in Papeete one day later," he smiled bitterly. "Do you think I really want to go there?"

The fourth passenger on board was Sam Kumler, a gentleman of leisure, of sorts. Sam had fallen into a small inheritance in his youth. Too meager to support him in the USA, it enabled him to survive in places like Mexico, Guatemala, and Tahiti, where he spent most of his life. He was a bit of a miser, and conspicuously void of aspiration. "I wouldn't give fifty bucks to learn Tahitian. They'd treat me like a native if I spoke their language," he explained. "I've never gone shark fishing," he would say, or "I've never been to Europe." Once he told me proudly, "I've never read anything of importance, and I don't miss it one iota." During the war years he had remained in Tahiti. "You wouldn't think I'd get myself mixed up in anything like that." When the war ended he wanted to return to the States, but it was impossible to obtain passage. One day a ship docked in Papeete and the steward fell ill. Sam took the vacancy and *worked* his way home as a waiter. He did of late, however, have a disquieting dilemma. While his money was locked in a trust fund, he felt the time was ripe to dig into his capital. "If only I could know *when* I'd kick the bucket, believe me, I'd work it out so beautifully. I'd spend my last buck the day I die."

The fifth passenger was Homer Morgan, a handsome, energetic young man. The son of an affluent Los Angeles family, he had enjoyed a fine upbringing–Beverly Hills High School, a brief Army Service in Europe toward the end of the war, and the University of Southern California. He owned a sailboat, drove a convertible, and dated pretty girls in Hollywood. The playboy life he led after graduating, however, did not satisfy him. Searching for adventure, he and a friend followed up an advertisement calling for a partnership in a shark fishing enterprise off Tahiti. They made an investment, but ended up with a shack on the beach and a lagoon full of fish. "I'd be darned if I was going to write home for dough," said Homer. Australia was next on the agenda. Homer's friend went ahead, and Homer was to follow on the next monthly steamer. But by the time the steamer arrived he had fallen in love with a beautiful Chinese-Polynesian girl. He was married in the big wooden house of his bride's huge and prominent family in Papeete, and he decided to make Tahiti his home. Tutoring English and initiating an English language program on Radio Tahiti (fifteen minutes a week), he was now returning from one of his periodic trips to the mainland. In the next half century, Homer would become a prosperous tourist entrepreneur, a part-time writer (*A Dinosaur in Paradise*), and one of Tahiti's most celebrated US expatriates.

As for me, the sixth passenger aboard, I was going to Tahiti on a film job. Freshly graduated from UCLA in film-making, it was time for me to gain experience in the field. This was not easy, the film companies being somewhat mistrustful of the first crop of graduates in this new academic discipline, and indeed our practical training was mostly in the documentary realm, not in dramatic films. One day a call came from Abe Mayer, a respected talent agent at MCA, Hollywood's largest artist agency. Rather than representing individual artists, MCA was famous for putting 'packages' together (like a book, a director, an actor, and a studio). Abe was a gentle, kindly man I had met several times before. "Say, how would you like to go to Tahiti?–yes, *TA*-hiti–documentary, right up your alley–local party, wealthy Frenchman, lived there all his life–he wants to make movies–no, not yet, he needs someone to teach him– yes, he's got equipment–no, no, *you* are going to direct, run the operation for a while–yeah, I'm flying down there myself– don't worry, we'll work it out–you'd like to kick it around?–you *could* drop by?–yes, an hour is fine." A peculiar proposition, not really what MCA was normally about, but Abe had a point: documentary *was* my alley. He didn't need to twist my arm.

A day before we reached our destination, we saw land. We were at the Western end of a collection of coral islands, the Tuamotus, extending well over a thousand miles of ocean. "There is no other group of islands so remote from any continent," wrote Nordhoff and Hall. Scattered clusters of dark blue coconut palms appeared on the horizon. Presently we were passing between two atolls, Makatea and Tikeahu, both visible in the distance on either side. The sight was strange and unfamiliar. Graceful palms here and there, white surf mildly battering the reefs but, paradoxically, no visible land, so flat were the islands. I felt like a thirsty desert traveler who sees an oasis and finds a mirage. That night we passed a ship in the distance, a copra schooner from Papeete. The two ships exchanged greetings, sounding their horns. It was good to know we were no longer alone in the universe. The next morning we arrived in Tahiti.

It was still dark when we awoke. The ship was still, the hum of its engines finally gone. Idly the *Waihemo* waited for the morning. A sweet tropical scent came to the cabin with each gust of wind from the land. There, in front, lay the jewel of the Pacific, majestic and awe-inspiring, a weird mountainous mass clad in misty, wet green. And behind us in the distance, like a dark painting, Tahiti's counterpart, the dim outline of Morea, rugged and forbidding.

When day broke the pilot arrived, accompanied by an official boarding party. Polite but excitable Frenchmen, dressed in colonial uniforms, checked each passenger's papers. The ship then entered the lagoon of Papeete through the natural pass, a break in the endless reef encircling the island. Not a hundred feet away, on the reef's edge, stood a young fisherman. His figure, strong and undaunted by the ship's entrance, remained a dark silhouette against the emptiness around him. He stood there, perplexed, as though saying, "When will you white men learn not to disturb my fish?"

Less than half an hour later we were docked at Papeete, the heart of Tahiti and capital of French Oceania. The arrival of a ship always caused great excitement on the island, and ours was no exception. The pier was packed with people; brown bodies simply clad, happy faces, and flowers everywhere. When the islanders came aboard to welcome the new arrivals, Abe Mayer was among them. He had arrived earlier on a small sea-plane from Hawaii, and the effects of an extended vacation were manifest on him. He placed a large *hei* of tiare blossoms on my neck, kissed me traditionally on both cheeks, and whispered confidentially, "the deal is on."

Gaston Guilbert, the man I had come to see, was the owner of the Oceanic Garage, situated on the main street near the port. A wooden structure in ill repair, it was cluttered with used crates and junk, the dusty walls decorated with faded prints of new model cars. Gaston, lean and slight of build, with dark hair and eyes set deep in his skull, was handsome in appearance. But his eyes were restless, and there was a tense nervousness in his manner. His handshake was ugly, wet and cold, and of his bitten fingernails there was hardly a remnant. Our introduction, in Abe's cheery ministration, was brief. Gaston hastily arranged for Tu, the taxi driver, to take me to *'Chez Rivnac,'* an aging bungalow pension along the lagoon, not far from Gaston's own residence. As we drove along the shaded asphalt road encircling the island, I wondered about the edgy nature of the man I had just met, starkly inconsistent with the serene environment we were passing.

No dwelling could have characterized the South Seas more than the simple hut allotted to me. Built of yellow bamboo with a palm-thatched roof, the front portion rested in the green shade of coconut palms, while the back, supported on poles, extended out over the beach. There were flowers in the hut: Tiare, white and sweet, like the ones I wore around my shoulders, Frangipani, large and strongly perfumed, and Aute, red and wild-looking. The door had no lock and remained open. Through the hanging palm-leaf shutters I could see the reef, within swimming distance, where the surf sprouted up in fountains of spume. Toward sunset Venus touched the glassy surface of the lagoon and left a thin white line approaching and almost touching me.

The first evening was memorable. Gaston threw a *luau* for the new arrivals. Among the guests were Abe, myself, Gaston's old acquaintance Sam Kumler, and Captain White as the guest of honor. A troupe of musicians entered with guitars, maracas, and an unceasing enthusiasm for Tahitian music. They were led by a well fed young vocalist, who earned her living as Gaston's laundry girl. The table, set with fruits and flowers, was a work of art, and the meal delicious. Gaston, however, was distant and quiet. As I soon learnt, he lived alone, and had little yearning for human company.

Gaston's home—it could easily be called a mansion—was an assortment of bungalows, laid out in orderly fashion in his well-kept residential plantation between the asphalt road encircling the island and the beach. Only two of the buildings, however, served for living. One was the spacious main house, in which the airy living room and Gaston's own quarters were located, and the other a house for guests. The living room featured a bar resembling a ship's interior. Several paintings of Tahiti by resident European artists hung on the few walls, and through the large openings lush tropical verdure shot up. Hundreds of brown baby lizards clung to the cream colored ceiling, baking motionless upside down in the heat. A nasty old toucan, displaying colorful but clipped feathers, walked freely about the house. It had been brought years ago from Mexico by Gaston's friend Sam Kumler, doubtless one of the few gifts Sam ever gave and Gaston ever received. Near the bar was a dining set, where Gaston had his lonely meals. A heavy ship's bell, heard well across the lagoon, sounded before a meal was served to summon Gaston to table.

From the main house a narrow concrete path, shaded by a thatch, led to a hut which served as kitchen. In it reigned an ancient, wrinkled Chinese cook, high voiced and deaf. Aki was his name, and no one knew how old he was or whence he came. On the whole island he had no friend or family. Gaston decided the old man wouldn't know what to do with a day off, and therefore never gave him one. It was Aki who rang the bell when dinner was ready, and it was he who served it. Aki was both fearful and strangely defiant of his master. When Gaston suddenly shrieked Aki's name, the startled old man would crouch and tremble. But Aki pronounced the kitchen taboo, and even Gaston lacked the daring to enter it. If Gaston was but a minute late to table, Aki would attack the bell with all the might of his slight body, until Gaston obediently took his seat and waited for the old man to halt his wrath.

The rest of the bungalows on the estate were used as playthings for Gaston's odd preoccupation with film-making. There was a tiny projection room, a small hut converted into a recording studio, and several storage huts with assorted equipment. Gaston was particularly proud to point to an elderly Tahitian whose job it was, "when not in production," to wash Gaston's cars. The man was Matahi, renowned for his famous portrayal in his youth of the unfortunate lover in F.W. Murnau's and Robert Flaherty's silent South Sea classic *Tabu* (Paramount Pictures, 1931). "A collector, that's what he is," said Sam Kumler, "Like my mother, she collects china. Gaston collects motion picture paraphernalia."

In the discussions about the proposed project we were

to do, Abe tried to steer Gaston toward a modest, realistic goal, perhaps a straightforward documentary capturing the unique allure and beauty of the islands. Gaston had his mind set on an epic production, which he named "Motu Ino" after a small islet he had once visited. He would not hear of any film project other than that. But he also argued that there was no girl pretty enough for the part, and that he intended to wait for a certain twelve-year old from the other side of the island to grow up and become his star. "Is there a script, or a story?" I inquired. "I don't need a script," Gaston replied, "I know it. I know everything in it. I don't need to write it." Dumbfounded as we were, the next day Gaston surprised us even more. "Of course there is a script," he said calmly. "I wrote it for five years. It's finished. It's *mimeographed*. But I am not showing it to anyone." He walked over to his desk, fingered through a stack of folders, picked one and waved it in the air. "Here, look how thick!" Carefully he put the volume into a drawer, kicked the drawer shut with his knee, and walked out triumphantly into the plantation. I noticed, however, that the drawer had not snapped shut when Gaston had rammed it. The book he had just waved was no script. It was an old automotive spare-parts catalogue.

In disbelief, Abe buried his crimson face in his hands. Although he had come to Tahiti primarily for an island holiday, this outcome was an insult to his professional competence. For me it was, alas, much worse. I had come for nothing. The next ship out of Tahiti was almost a month away—a freighter to New York, of all places, via the Panama Canal. Short of choices, I booked passage and proceeded to wait out my forced internment in paradise.

It turned out to be one of the happiest and most enlightening episodes of my life. There was much to learn on the island. It was taboo, for example, to wake someone when asleep. If urgent, as is wont to be in our age, the acceptable way was to hold a flower gently near the sleeping person's nose. Life on the island was unbelievably uncomplicated. Food was abundant, want was unknown. The lagoon teemed with fish, and coconuts, when ripe, fell from the sky. Most Tahitians played the guitar, and their music was cheerful and bright. Undoubtedly it was this Garden of Eden quality that fired Western imagination ever since Captain Wallis, on the H.M.S. *Duff,* threw anchor in Tahiti in 1767.

Once, while photographing an elderly fisherman at his work, someone asked me if I knew who the man was. "No," I said, "he just looks right." "It is the son of Paul Gaugin," was the comeback. I was baffled. Should I have felt pity for an abandoned, uneducated wastrel, or esteem for a man clearly at peace with himself?

Quinn's Bar in 'downtown' Papeete opened its doors to the public at nine o'clock every morning. During the forenoon hours business was slow; a keen owner might have remained closed until later in the day. But Quinn's was more than a bar. It was a refuge for the troubled, a sanctuary for the unfortunate. The heart and soul of Quinn's sociability was Nabuco the waitress. Middle-aged and hoarse, a guitar always within her reach, there was wisdom in her eyes and authority in her voice. People in distress came to her to seek advice, and she knew how to set things right. For local color and a bit of drama, there was no better place to find it than at Quinn's. This morning Tita was there, Teave's wife from across the island. Tita was 'fiu' with her husband. "Today he will come," said Nabuco, "he can't go on fishing forever." "Even if he walked in now, I wouldn't go home," said Tita, "that's final." Oh yes, you would, thought Nabuco, but said, "Have a beer, Tita, he's not here yet, anyway." Teave knew where to look for his wife, and upon arriving in Papeete on the morning bus, walked straight to Quinn's. He strode over to Tita and stood beside her. "Let's go home," he said quietly. "I'm not coming," she answered. "A little later, then," said Teave gently and sat down at the other end of the bar. "Nabuco," he shouted in anger, "One beer."

Two people with whom I became friendly in Papeete were John and Mary Caldwell, who sailed into the bay one afternoon on their little ketch, the *Tropic Seas*, after many months at sea. They had come from Los Angeles, and were on their way to Australia. Astonishingly, with them aboard were their two children, aged five and two, and as if this were not enough, Mary was in her eighth month of pregnancy. With due respect for their courage, there was a feeling, even among the small group of yachtsmen moored along the bay who had accomplished the incredible feat of crossing the Pacific, that having such young children aboard was a bit reckless. Mary Caldwell answered this reproach. They had lost one baby to a virus infection in America, and the smaller boy had a dangerous immune deficiency. "If this is our fate among doctors in the civilized world, I am not afraid to have my children on the boat," she said, "There is no Virus X at sea." While in Tahiti, Mary gave birth to a healthy baby, and John eventually wrote a book about their passage, *Family at Sea,* (Little Brown, New York, 1956), and became even more successful with *Desperate Voyage* (Sheridan House, New York, 1991).

One of the most splendid young men I met in Papeete was light-footed, industrious Ben Bambridge. A paramedic at the Pacific Tropical Diseases Project, he drove around the island in a white jeep, visiting households, taking blood samples, collecting larvae, and enforcing mosquito control measures. Tahiti had a high rate of infection from filariasis, a mosquito-borne worm which attacks the lymphatic system, ultimately leading to elephantiasis, and Ben was the frontrunner of this health campaign. He spoke fluent English, though he had never left the island. I spent a lovely Sunday at Ben's country house, built of stone and covered in tropical foliage. Ben's wife prepared raw fish in coconut milk, Tahiti's specialty, and with their three boys we climbed the dense mountainside to their hidden waterfall. Ben's family history was remarkable. His grandfather was the son of an English missionary, Thomas Bambridge, who had married a Tahitian girl. Ben's grandmother was the daughter of an English pirate, Tapscott, who had abducted a wife from the Cannibal Islands. Ben's father married a Tahitian who had Spanish ancestry. And Ben's own wife was half Chinese. Ben told me of an American he had met, who had prompted him to search into his ancestry. "I wrote it all down for him. He said he would get it published, but I never heard from him again. His name was Michener. He said he was a writer." Upon my return to civilization, I quickly found that Michener had kept his word, in *Return to Paradise* (Mass Market Paperback, New York, 1950).

They say you must cry when you leave Tahiti. Life started early that morning. The whole town seemed to be at the waterfront. On board, busy custom officials shouted, and porters perspired under heavy trunks. Along the dock old women selling *heis* ran out of stock and pooled their skills to hastily make new ones. Islanders came aboard to say farewell, and I too received visitors beyond my expectations. Tu the taxi driver came aboard and put a *hei* on my shoulders. A kiosk woman from whom I had once bought shell necklaces also brought a hei. Homer Morgan, John Caldwell, and Ben Bambridge, came with *heis* and stayed until the ship sailed. The two Mormon lads came by. "We'll soon be off to one of the Tuamotus," they said. "There's no church there as yet, but we hope to start one." Soon stewards with bored faces walked along the decks, ringing their bells, to which visitors paid scant attention. Abe Mayer came up with *heis*. "See you at the office," he said encouragingly. He was due to take the seaplane to Honolulu in a few days. Sam Kumler came to shake hands too, although he brought no *hei* with him. Gaston Guilbert was not to be seen. He was known to avoid coming to departures.

Finally the ship started to move, so slowly it was hardly noticeable at first. Spontaneously the people on shore broke out in a farewell song, *Mauru Uru*. This was the moment when many reached for their handkerchiefs, for it marked the very instant when the present turns into the past before your eyes. Passengers began to throw their *heis* overboard in the direction of their loved ones. A pretty Tahitian girl in the crowd, wearing a white skirt, waved to someone near me. She was the quiet young chambermaid at *Chez Rivnac*. I looked round to see whom she was seeing off, but no one responded to her signals. When I looked back at her, she laughed and pointed at me. I was astonished. "Thank you," I yelled out, and then, quite touched, "What is your name?" We were nearly too far. Maybe she understood, for she answered something, perhaps "Mo-e." "Mo-e!" I called out, but she heard me no more.

The ship's retreat was painfully slow. For a long time people on shore stood waving, but long after most had dispersed, Mo-e was still there. She bade me farewell in true Polynesian fashion, slowly waving her arms up and sideways. I waved back.

No one felt the finality of departure as profoundly as the island women. It was like in the old days, when the men left in their outrigger canoes to brave the endless ocean, and the women, so it was said, knew who would return and who would be lost at sea. By now I could no longer see Mo-e's arms, and soon the white spot, her skirt, was also lost to sight. Tahiti had been kind and tolerant and gentle. I was grateful for having been there, and I knew, like those legendary women, that I would probably not see this paradise again. I felt the tears rise in me. I was crying.

We were now beyond the reef. The sea was choppy. I threw my last *hei* overboard.

Happy islanders

A Tahitian fisherman, allegedly the son of Paul Gaugin

Tahitian Hit: Saka Saka E Mamma

8

"Fincho"

Patrick Akponu, the lead in "Fincho"

One night in 1954, at the home of my London relatives Boria (Boris) and Rena Behrman, Boria showed some 8mm color footage he had taken at their timber concession in Nigeria. The Behrman family had been in the timber business for several generations, still in the 'old country' (Latvia), and the Nigeria concession was a new extension of their UK firm, Finch & Company. What I saw there was formidable. Giant trees were being felled in the jungle, and hundreds of bare-handed African workers were pulling the heavy trunks through the mud.

It did not take me long to realize that this could well be a starting point for an extraordinary documentary, and perhaps even more than that. For some time I had felt a strong desire to move from the short film, my medium hitherto, to full-length form. If I could find a human story to fit into the tree felling process, perhaps the chance of realizing this notion was here on a silver platter. Boria generously said I could stay in one of the bungalows built for the white staff at the concession and film whatever I wanted. Admittedly, it would be foolhardy to go script-less into the unknown, but therein lay the challenge.

And so, toward the end of the Central African rainy season in 1955, equipped with a 16mm Arriflex camera, a portable sound recording device, and a reasonable amount of Kodachrome color film, I set out on a flight to Lagos, the capital of Nigeria at the time, and from there, mostly over unpaved and ill-maintained dirt roads, passing through two enormous clusters of mud huts, Ibadan and Benin City, to the Finch timber concession in the far-away Kingdom of the *Olowo* ('Ruler') of *Owo*.

The bungalow I was given at the concession was spacious, though the heat was unbearable. In the outdoor kitchen behind, an attendant called 'house-boy' or 'boy' for short, no matter what his age, was on duty twenty four hours. Plagued at night by mosquitoes infiltrating my net, I could hear the house-boy in the kitchen slapping his back and shoulders incessantly, hunting the malaria-carrying little devils. He did not have the luxury of a mosquito net, nor did he have a bed.

With time I got used to the heat and humidity, and the

mosquitoes at night. I almost managed to enjoy an imaginary air-conditioner before falling asleep: someone had kindheartedly handed me a copy of Sir Edmund Hillary's and Tenzing Norgay's *The Conquest of Everest*, which kept me cool throughout my stay on the concession.

In Owo I met the Olowo, a big man amply robed in a manner quite inconsistent with the climate. His palace was a large two-storey mud structure painted white, and it seemed densely populated. "Who are all these people?" I inquired. "These are the King's wives and children," I was told.

Although I examined everything I saw as a potential focal point for the film's story, I soon realized that neither the harsh colonial exploitation of the natives, nor the social hierarchy of traditional African rulers, would be my anchor. It was the tree-felling enterprise itself, and the impact this had on those caught in its advance.

My guide and mentor on the concession was an Englishman named Tony Lewis, the second-in-command at Finch and an old hand in the African timber trade. To the Africans he spoke a kind of broken English, which I thought at first to be his own invention, but soon discovered this was genuine 'Pidgin,' a simplified English language in use there, delightful and humorous, and the only way the three main ethnic groups in Nigeria—Yoruba, Ibo, and Hausa—could communicate with each other. I promptly decided that wherever possible this would be the film's language.

"I *de* go" was present tense. "I *done* go" was past. "I *go* go" was future. "*Make you* go bringam" was a command. Just a minute was "Wait small." Dialogue, such as "Nah whei he dei?" (Now, where is he?) when answered by "He dei fo house," referred to either male, female, or neuter. Father was "small fahda," while "big fahda" meant grandfather. "Plenty palavah" was big trouble. Great satisfaction: "He de tickle me propa." Disbelief: "Na lie! You think you go deceive me like small boy?" Two Africans talking to a white man: "Sah. Dis man, he be my brudda." "Oh really? Same mudda same fahda?" "No sah, my brudda."

A most impressive man was the concession's CEO. A WW2 ex-military man with a hyphenated name, Gordon Parry-Holroyd seemed the quintessence of gentleman and servant of Empire. He had a family and a cottage in the Midlands of England, but after the war preferred the wilds of Africa to life in civilization. He was a mix of tenacity and gentleness, reminiscent of Conrad's Lord Jim, with a tinge of a Heart of Darkness.

Slowly the story I was looking for began to materialize in my mind. The protagonist would be a young African, torn between the preservation of age-old traditions and the acceptance of encroaching modernization. His final choice would ultimately be his embracing the modern world.

To tell the story, other characters would have to be created. Representing the conservative view would be the village's spiritual leader, the feared and angry jujuman. Pitted against him would be the young schoolmaster, who champions progress and enlightenment. Into the village enters a white timber extractor, Mistah Finch, who persuades the village chief to allow the felling of trees, but is refused permission to hire local labor. Our protagonist, eager to marry his girl but perpetually short of the needed dowry to buy her from her father, starts working for the white man in spite of the proscription. Called now 'Fincho' because he is 'dancing around with the white man,' he becomes something of a leader, many other young men joining him. But when new earth-moving equipment is brought in to replace the local labor, violence is about to erupt against the white man. It is Fincho who succeeds in calming the uprising and renewing the work, thus bringing about momentous change in his community. He even triggers an understanding between the jujuman and the schoolmaster.

In creating characters, it is important, I think, to avoid what is known as one-dimensional representation. Thus the Jujuman, whose main function in the film is to scold and to rebuke, should be shown also to possess a more benevolent side–easing pain, for instance, when leading a village funeral, or calling the Gods to bring rain during a drought. The schoolmaster, when translating for the chief, although wishing in his heart that working for the white man would be permitted, conscientiously and eloquently explains to Mr. Finch why the villagers cannot abandon their traditional way of life.

In the numerous scenes between Fincho and his girl, there is, as there must be, a constant change in the respective positions of the two. Every scene between them thus reflects a minute alteration from the scene before. In the beginning Fincho is determined to work for the white man, while his girl is firmly against it. Toward the end the situation is reversed, and it is the girl who persuades Fincho to return to work.

The film would alternate between scenes of direct dialogue and voice-over narration, and the narrator would be Fincho himself. Many of the scenes would show local color, like at the market, or at the Chief's court, and the awesome tree-felling process would be followed in detail. Some scenes, like Fincho's engagement negotiations between the two families, or the naming ceremony of his first-born, were actually written out in detail by the cast and crew on rainy days when shooting was impractical.

It is my conviction that any work of fiction contains, or should contain, a message, a moral if you like, implied or explicit, that makes the story relevant. Writing this account more than fifty years after the event, I would be hard put to defend the story's point of view vehemently today. Deplorably, the price of deforestation, and the resulting ills to society and to the planet, has proven to be much higher than at first conceived, yet sadly the process goes on as before.

Clearly, a lot of thought and time would be required to turn a skeleton of a story into a detailed plan, a full screenplay with dialogue written out. Simultaneously a production crew had to be trained, the actors cast, scene locations determined, costumes and props chosen, a story board devised, and a shooting schedule worked out, before shooting could actually begin.

The production crew, kept to a minimum, consisted of four young local men who, naturally, had no previous connection to film-making. Samson Orhokpocha, a natural organizer, became a sort of production manager. Michael Nwaitabo, whose job was to carry the camera and tripod, became assistant cameraman. Sound recordist was Sunday Obende. He recorded the dialogue scenes, albeit as cue tracks only, for later dubbing in the studio. He also recorded the felling of trees, which sounded like heavy cloth being torn slowly, followed after the fall by a symphony of terrified animals and birds. Although sound effects were later added in the studio, Sunday's work was extraordinary in itself. The fourth member of the crew was Rufus Atangbayila, who carried light-weight tin-foil reflectors to lighten the shadows, particularly in close-up shots. The whole picture would be shot in daylight, so no electric lighting equipment would be needed. Rather, because lighting equipment was simply out of the question, the film would have to be shot in daylight, and limited to 'exteriors' only.

Casting was not always easy or smooth, at times illuminating the tribal atmosphere of life deep in the jungle. Early in the production, looking for a suitable Fincho, I found a healthy-looking young man on the concession, named Aladdi. We shot some tests with him, which were sent to a London film lab for development. It took weeks before a print came back, during which Aladdi fell mysteriously ill, and soon died. Rumor had it that someone had wished him dead, presumably over an issue with a woman, and that he had died of a juju. Having been a popular figure in the community, Aladdi's death was much talked-about. One fellow on a trip to Benin City said he had seen him there alive, and another had met and spoken with him in far-away Ibadan. Both reported that Aladdi looked good and was well dressed, and would soon come back to close the account with his murderer.

At the compound stood a large board, built of wooden planks painted white, which served as a movie screen, and some distance away was a hut with an old 16mm projector in it. From time to time rented feature films were shown to the workers as a bonus. When the test including Aladdi arrived, I decided to run it for the crew after dark, so they could see what they were actually doing. Word leaked fast, and quickly several hundred Africans assembled there. It was a still, moonless night, and when Aladdi's image appeared on the board, in full color, a terrified hush fell over the audience. Someone screamed, women hid their babies, others fled. "He finally came back," my crew explained to me as we dismantled the test, "and tonight he will find the man who killed him." My remonstration that it was only his image we saw, not him, convinced no one. In truth, it was I who felt a bit uncomfortable that evening.

When Aladdi had fallen ill, and I had suggested that he see a doctor, he said that only a black man could cure him. When his condition deteriorated, and I offered to take him to the mission hospital, half a day's drive away, he said, "If I go to a white doctor, I shall die." I persisted, perhaps too strongly, and when we arrived at the small hospital, the only doctor, a youngish German with a heavy accent, said I should leave Aladdi there for a few days.

After some ten days without a sign of Aladdi, I drove to the hospital again. "Good zat you come," the doctor welcomed me, "your man is just now dying." Indeed, in the ward Aladdi was about to expire. "What of?" I demanded. "We gave him every test," the doctor explained, "All negative. There is a lot we don't know about African diseases and juju. And we cannot perform autopsies because we have no refrigeration. Do you want to take the body back with you or should we bury him in the mission graveyard here?" I stayed till after the death and the burial, and when I got back to the outpost, there was no need to say anything. Mysteriously, everyone already knew the sad news, and had known all along this would be the outcome.

Whether by power of the juju or plain coincidence, during the night of the screening a thunderstorm broke out over the outpost, and next morning half the compound's thatched roofs were gone. The crew informed me that Aladdi had been there and had found his killer. I must admit I felt a shadow of relief on learning that the finger had not been pointed at me. After that, Aladdi no longer returned to the living.

The role of Fincho finally went to Patrick Akponu, a conductor on the Lagos-Owo bus line, which was actually an open truck.

He was a proud young tribesman from Onitsha, on the Niger River. Would he like to work on a film? Yes, he would. Could he read English? Yes, he had gone to school until his father died, though his education had never been completed. A week later he came to the concession. He wore no shoes and ate with his fingers, and he was natural and friendly. While learning his lines, he suddenly exclaimed, "I did this before, in the village school." "You did what?" I asked. "Shakespeare," he said. And while I marveled at the sound of this word coming from his lips, he stood up, looked about as if confronting an audience, and said boldly, *"Friends, Romans, countrymen, lend me your ears,"* and broke into a hearty laugh. At that moment I knew I was lucky, and indeed it became a pleasure to work with him.

For the role of Fincho's Girl I found a charming, expressive young girl, named Amukpue. Only when I handed her the dialogue lines, it turned out she was illiterate. Her role went to a young vocalist from a band in Lagos, who could read English, memorize her lines, and act them out without effort. Her name was Comfort Ajilo.

Casting the White Man was a bit of a problem at first, the supply of candidates being so limited. The only man who looked the part was the concession's CEO, who I feared would decline, considering his status and responsibilities. I was also concerned that Boria would not be overjoyed to find his top man having become an actor. When in desperation I turned to Gordon Parry-Holroyd, he accepted with great pleasure, and filled his part conscientiously and convincingly.

To play the Jujuman I approached the real fellow, who spoke no English. His part, however, did not require it, Yoruba being sufficient, and it would add authenticity to his character. The problem arose when after several rehearsals of a shot, as soon as he'd hear the camera roll, he would freeze completely and just stand still. One of the onlookers, a lean middle-aged man, suddenly jumped in impatiently to show him what to do. His name was Adebayo Fuwa, and in the end he got the part.

Two cast members actually played themselves, the schoolmaster, Bashiru Abibu, a bright and obliging fellow who invested in his part the same commitment he had for his profession; and Chief Adedigba, the village chief. There were also Mistah Finch's driver, Gabriel Adebisi, forever busy polishing the boss's Land Rover, Fincho's Father Pa George Agho, the Girl's Father Augustine Ihonde, and a white woman on the compound who played Finch's wife joining him in the jungle, a non-speaking and therefore a non-credited part.

Those were days before zoom lenses, and if one wanted a moving shot, one could only pan sideways or tilt up and down. To heighten intimacy by moving in slowly, imperceptibly, on a close-up or a two-shot, one needed a dolly. We built one, using two bicycles with a platform between them.

Shooting the felling of trees was particularly dramatic. The fellers always knew which way the giant trees would fall, and directed us where to place the camera for safety. Once, however, their calculations fell short. I was filming the beginning of a fall, concentrating on the trunk at the tree's base and expecting it to fall away from us, when suddenly, amid frenzied shouting, camera and tripod were grabbed away from me as the huge mass above was swinging down toward us. There was barely time to escape when, like in a nightmare, I discovered my foot was stuck in the undergrowth. It was only a split second between the crew pulling me free from my shoe and the mammoth trunk hitting the ground. *A Kingdom for a Horse?* A Life for a Shoe.

All in all I spent six months 'in the interior.' Except for the test with Aladdi, I saw no rushes in Africa, relying rather on the lab reports from London than having the material shipped out. I left many friends in the Kingdom of Owo, black and white. Particularly Fincho remained dear to my heart. I sent him several packages and books, and hoped he would advance to a better life than he had before. This did not come to pass. Within a month or two, one of my letters to him was returned with an official stamp, 'Deceased.'

The next stage was the editing and finishing of the film. This took place in Los Angeles, where I had an assistantship teaching film at UCLA, my Alma Mater. Editing was made easy, as I had kept the entire film on story board, which I had updated daily during shooting. All I had to do now was arrange the shots in sequence, and 'fine cut.' I rounded up several Nigerian students at the University for the dubbing of voices, and was elated, amid raucous laughter, to practice Pidgin again. The dialogue and the narration of Fincho's voice I dubbed myself. Even the short Fincho Song, words written by well-known lyricist Sid Robin, I sang and recorded with a small Mexican band. As befits an almost budget-less home production, I cut the negative myself.

Film, I believe, can be made more suggestive by the use of images and sounds not necessarily connected to the scene at hand, much like metaphors in language. When, for example, Fincho and his girl, alone in an empty riverbed, discuss their future, a close shot of a tropical bird overhearing their conversation appears momentarily. This is not a planned shot in the screenplay but an editing idea, and the short clip of the bird is purchased from a 'stock library' in the film capital. When Fincho, riding with the timber down the river, reaches the ocean freighter, which he sees for the first time in his life, we hear the big ship sounding its horn. This would not happen in reality, but the sound effect adds a dimension to the scene.

A kindly Hollywood composer, Alexander Laszlo, offered to compose and record an original score for the film. Truthfully, I was not convinced that a symphonic score was the most appropriate addition to the film, thinking a small combo or a single African instrument would be better. Eventually I was persuaded that a big orchestration would add stature to the film, an assumption I still question in my mind to this day. In any event, I had brought with me recordings of what was known as *Lagos Highlife*, and Laszlo adapted the syncopated rhythms with his own melody as the *Leitmotiv* of the film, including that of the Fincho Song. For the title background sheets, art student Sheldon Schoneberg, who went on to become a well-known artist, drew actual key scenes from the film in ink and color, to familiarize the viewer subliminally with coming events.

The final cut ran seventy five minutes, a bit short perhaps for a feature, but better, I thought, than dragging it out another five or six minutes and slowing down the pace. My shooting ratio (the ratio between exposed stock to that actually used in the finished film) was 3:1, an efficient rate, made possible no doubt by the use of a detailed story board, and also by the necessity to be prudent. The net running time of finished film achieved during the shooting period was about one minute per shooting day, not a bad yield at all.

Deeply moved at the time by the enormously popular singer and black activist Harry Belafonte, I boldly wrote him to ask if he would consider adding an introduction to the film. To my surprise he responded. He would gladly see the film, and suggested that I come to Las Vegas, where he was appearing nightly in one of the leading hotels, and show him the film. Packing a 'Movieola' (a somewhat bulky editing machine with a small screen) and the 'work-print' of the not quite finished film into my car, I drove to Nevada. Belafonte saw the film in his hotel room and agreed on the spot to cooperate. We made a date at a small New York studio a few weeks hence, and filmed Belafonte delivering a short address I had prepared. He did this entirely on a voluntary basis.

My Nigerian gamble thus worked out beyond my wildest dreams. After the film was completed, a most touching accolade came in the form of an unsolicited letter written by three leading Hollywood figures to the Production Head of 20th Century Fox, calling his attention to my work. The three renowned signatories were screenwriter and playwright Norman Corwin, director Fred Zinnemann, and composer Bernard Herrmann. I shall forever remain grateful for their munificence. Lastly, I also deepened a lifelong friendship with the Behrmans, who had made it all possible.

Sound recordist Sunday Obende adjusting levels for a shot

Directing Fincho and his girl in preparation of a dolly shot

Sam Zebba

Lagos Highlife

Harry Belafonte introducing the film "Fincho"

9

Anna and I

Dr. Anna Wildikann, in Jerusalem (Eidelman)

I met Anna Wildikann during the middle years of World War II, when I was in my late teens. My mother was undergoing minor surgery at the Hadassah Hospital in Jerusalem, and I had come up from Tel-Aviv, where we lived, to visit her. The other bed in my mother's room was occupied by a somewhat mysterious lady doctor who had come to be treated in Palestine all the way from French Equatorial Africa, Hadassah being one of the few medical facilities left accessible due to the war, and the nearest to her remote mission station in the Gabon, up the vast Ogowe River.

That lady in the next bed was, of course, Anna Wildikann, and it quickly transpired that she and my mother had quite astonishing common links. Both were originally from Riga, and both had left Europe in the early 1930's. Incredibly, my kindergarten teacher in Riga, before my parents immigrated to Palestine, had been a certain Fraulein Wildikann, none other than Anna's sister Naama, who perished in the Holocaust, and whom even I vaguely remembered.

Anna's story was highly unconventional, almost bizarre. The daughter of a medical family, Anna studied medicine in Jena and in Heidelberg, two of the last few universities in Germany still open to foreigners and Jews, and upon graduation attended a lecture by the great organist, musicologist, theologian, philosopher, and physician Dr. Albert Schweitzer, who came to Europe periodically to raise funds for his unique mission hospital in Lambarene. Intuitively aware, perhaps, of the approaching catastrophe in Europe, or filled with her newly acquired obligation to cure human suffering wherever needed, or perhaps fascinated by the extraordinary personality of the lecturer, Anna decided to join Dr. Schweitzer's small medical team at his African outpost. There she remained for well over a decade, dedicating her best years to his mission, until ill-health required her to seek medical attention nearer civilization.

Anna had a quiet, patient air about her, not only while hospitalized, but later too. She spoke in a soft, relaxed voice, at once modest yet self-assured. True perhaps to her profession, she was both impartial observer and incisive diagnostician. Upon recovery from her operation, she decided to abandon Africa and remain in Palestine, but the British Authorities refused to extend her stay and, left without options, she went back to Lambarene.

Luckily for me, during the few weeks before her departure, Anna came to stay at my mother's apartment, and thus a small aperture into the world of Albert Schweitzer, and to that of Anna herself, opened up for me and made an indelible impact. The idea of going out on a quest to uncharted lands and extend a helping hand to those of a different civilization fascinated me. Anna was also a dedicated photographer, a growing passion of mine at the time, and one day she invited me to take pictures together in the Old City of Jerusalem. Her camera was rather antiquated, but she taught me the very essence of photography: how and what to look for. The studies I made that day of the Tower of David and the close-ups of Bedouin women and Arab vendors, black & white in those days before color photography came into use, were among the best shots I ever caught.

A few years later Anna returned to Palestine, this time on a legitimate 'capitalist' immigrant certificate. Obtaining such a document from the British involved depositing a considerable sum of money into the mandate coffers, and Anna must have spent a goodly portion of her resources to acquire it. Upon arrival, Anna quickly found her way to the British internment camp of Atlit, near Haifa, where Holocaust survivors, caught by the Royal Navy as they tried to reach the shores of Palestine, were incarcerated, in harsh and overcrowded conditions. There, as a volunteer medical officer, she tended the sick, doing what she was best qualified to do: working with grossly insufficient supplies and inadequate facilities. Were it someone else, this might have evoked sensations of sweet revenge toward those who had deported her, but to Anna, I am convinced, such sentiments were foreign. Ironically, it was but a few months after her arrival that the British withdrew and the State of Israel was declared, implementing the fundamental Law of Return, by which every Jew had the right to come and settle in Israel.

When under the new Israeli government the Atlit camp was cleared, Anna took up a position at the Hadassah Hospital in Jerusalem, where she had once been a patient. She settled in a small apartment in Rehavia, a comfortable residential quarter, and became an active member of Jerusalem's cultural circle. Her apartment, however, more than being a home, was a veritable museum and library in miniature, dedicated to Albert Schweitzer and to Anna's days in Lambarene. There were rare and just published volumes by and about Schweitzer, native sculptures in wood and ivory, some made by ex-patients of hers, many photographs of the hospital and of Schweitzer, manuscripts and letters. Anna wrote much about Lambarene, also in conjunction with Schweitzer, such as the little volume *The Story of My Pelican,* text by Schweitzer, photographs by Anna, which came out in many languages. Periodically Anna would travel to Europe, to medical conferences, to her publishers, and at times to meet Schweitzer himself, as she did when he received the Nobel Peace Prize in Oslo in 1953.

Anna had clear blue eyes and a fair complexion, and beautifully sculpted hands, yet she wore no make-up and dressed conservatively without regard for fashion. Never did I see her in the company of a man, and the notion of a romantic involvement seemed irrelevant to her, or else deeply concealed and zealously guarded. We never spoke about things like that, naturally, and in this Anna remained a bit of an enigma to me.

Imperceptibly, perhaps unconsciously, I found myself following Anna's footsteps. From the day I photographed those indigenous portraits in the Old City, my attitude to our Arab neighbors mellowed. Belonging as I did to the generation fated to fight the Germans, the British, and the Arabs, there was not much room left for compassion. Anna changed that in me, without saying a word, perhaps even without knowing it. While at film school in California I too, like Anna, went into the wilds, and upon graduating in the early 50's I felt ready to embark on a singular and noteworthy project: a documentary feature of the Schweitzer hospital in Lambarene.

When I approached The Albert Schweitzer Fellowship, a New York organization raising funds for the hospital, I was dumbfounded to learn that the Fellowship discouraged exposing documentation of the hospital, both because the facility was antiquated, never having been upgraded since its founding in 1913, and because of Schweitzer's legendary ethic of 'Reverence for Life,' which allowed chickens and stray monkeys to roam freely through the wards. If people saw this, the Fellowship seemed to fear, donations would cease.

I decided to give the idea another try, and approached the great man himself. A meeting was set up for me at Schweitzer's home in Guensbach, where he stayed during the summer. Schweitzer greeted me cordially, and invited me into his comfortable Biedermeier style living room. In his mid-seventies, Schweitzer was a big, impressive man, with a strong deep voice. I sensed right away, however, that the meeting was doomed. With his signature mustache, dressed in classic nineteenth-century fashion, he might have been a character in a period play. Schweitzer had hardly ever seen a movie, much less a documentary. The notion of him becoming a film actor, which he was certain would be required, seemed ludicrous to him. Assuming I was a medical man, he proposed that I join his staff in Lambarene, and he was visibly disappointed when he realized I was not a doctor. Before I left, however, Schweitzer autographed a photo for me, a prized possession I still display on my harpsichord at home in Tel-Aviv.

In 1955, amid wide publicity, a new book appeared, titled *The World of Albert Schweitzer*, by New York photographer Erica Anderson. It contained stunning and revealing shots of Schweitzer and of his hospital. On one of my stops in New York I asked to visit Ms. Anderson, and was genially invited to her studio. I was struck by Erica's resemblance to Anna. She spoke in a similar manner, slow and kindly, and with the same respect and awe toward Schweitzer as Anna had shown. Erica's roomy loft, rather in a state of disarray, was filled with photos of Schweitzer and the hospital. Readily she told me of the many times she had been to Lambarene over the years. She had even switched to using a movie camera, but her lack of film experience and Schweitzer's lack of enthusiasm for a film did not give her much hope. Only after I had left her studio, it occurred to me that photographs other than those of Schweitzer had been conspicuously absent in her surroundings. I could not help wondering where the thin line between professional interest and true infatuation rested. Erica continued her extended visits to Schweitzer, and completed her film in 1958. She obtained Schweitzer's permission to release it, and won the Academy Award for Best Documentary Feature that year.

In a totally coincidental way, Anna's life story continued to revisit me. In 1956 a book came out titled *The Nun's Story*, by Kathryn Hulme, and became an instant bestseller. Hulme, an American memoirist and author, told the story of a young

Belgian woman who became a nun, and was sent out as a nurse to a mission hospital in the Congo, where she was assigned to assist an opinionated lay surgeon. She found satisfaction in her work at the mission, which was not without peril, until a bout of tuberculosis forced her to return to Europe for treatment. Cured, she was allowed back to her station, and returned to Africa with renewed enthusiasm. Having discovered, however, the cruel devastation caused by the Germans in WW2, in which her physician father, tending wounded civilians, was indiscriminately killed, she could no longer reconcile her vows of universal compassion with her feelings of abhorrence and condemnation. She asked to be relieved of her vows and left Africa and the Convent.

It would be futile to deny the uncanny parallel between Anna's narrative and that of the book's fictitious 'Sister Luke.' The two were about the same age, for both it was compassion that led them to Africa, and for both—the unpardonable horrors of the war that guided them back. Even more astonishing was the fairly unpublicized fact that the model for Hulme's protagonist was a real person, a certain Marie Louise Habets, whom Hulme had met when both were nurses at a Displaced Persons camp in Poland immediately after the war, about the time Anna was working in Atlit.

Hollywood did not stand idly by. Warner Brothers bought the rights to the book and appointed Academy Award Winner Fred Zinnemann to direct the picture. Playwright Robert Anderson (*Tea and Sympathy*) wrote the screenplay, and Audrey Hepburn was cast as Sister Luke, with Peter Finch as Dr. Fortunati. The 1959 film was shot in Belgium, in Rome, and in the Belgian Congo, and was one of the most prestigious and expensive productions of its time. Zinnemann, who had seen my work from Brazil and Nigeria, chose me to be Second Unit Director, and so the great privilege fell to me, this time on the banks of the immense River Congo, to take part in the recreation of a life story which, thanks to my knowing Anna, was familiar to me long before *The Nun's Story* was written.

After Anna retired from Hadassah, she remained a beacon of kindness and hope in Jerusalem, working with underprivileged school-children, and often lecturing on her days in Lambarene. Eventually, her health deteriorating, she moved to a retirement home in Haifa, where she had relatives in the medical profession, and where she finally died in 1987, aged eighty six.

Albert Schweitzer died in Lambarene in 1965, aged ninety. His wife Helene Bresslau, a Jewess four years his junior, died in 1957, after forty five years of marriage. Their daughter Rhena, an only child, took over the hospital after her father's death, and like him lived to the age of ninety. She was married and had children and grandchildren, and she died in 2009.

Sadly, the others also are no more. Photographer Erica Anderson died in 1976, aged sixty two. Author Kathryn Hulme, born in San Francisco in 1900, died on the island of Maui in Hawaii in 1981, with Marie Louise Habets, the original ex-nun, at her bedside. The two women had lived together since the war. Marie Louise herself, born in Belgium, remained in Maui and died there five years later, one year before Anna's death.

Vienna-born Fred Zinnemann, whose *Nun's Story* won eight Academy Awards and numerous other distinctions died, after a brilliant career, in London in 1997. American-born Robert Anderson, the screenwriter, died in Manhattan in 2009, aged ninety one. The captivating Audrey Hepburn, born in Belgium, died at sixty three in Switzerland, where she had lived. Actor Peter Finch, born in London, and having served during the war, of all places, in the British Forces in Palestine, died in Beverly Hills in 1977.

My professor at UCLA and lifelong friend Dr. Kurt Bergel, who encouraged me to seek out Dr. Schweitzer, died in Orange, California, in 2001. After leaving UCLA, he founded the Albert Schweitzer Institute at Chapman College, and directed it well beyond his retirement.

I never made it to the Ogowe, but came close with my work in Nigeria and in the Congo. The three African countries involved, European colonies then, have long since won independence. Their names were changed, and their borders randomly redrawn, not without bloodshed. The names of the three great rivers—the Ogowe, the Niger, and the Congo—alone remained the same as they were then, unaltered to this day.

Albert Schweitzer waiting to be called on stage to deliver his keynote address at the Goethe bi-centennial celebration, Aspen, Colorado, 1949

The Nun's Story production shot. Director Fred Zinnemann in center, wearing hat. Stanleyville, Belgian Congo, 1958. (Photo Courtesy Zinnemann)

10

Firebird

"Firebird" braving the seas

One day in the late 1970's, my good friend Itz (short for Yitzhak Gvirzman), a successful Tel-Aviv architect, suggested that we both take a course in, of all things, sailing. Itz and his wife Shosh lived along the sea front near the Hilton Hotel, and Itz had observed a young fellow on the beach putting together a wooden shack in the sand and beginning to market a course in sailing, with the implausible vision of establishing a fully-fledged

Marina right there. Not like Itz at all, to be taken in by such a grandiose proposition, and as for me, writing my doctorate at the time and attending an orchestra conducting class at the Music Academy, I wasn't keen to take on new projects just then.

Nevertheless, two weeks later Itz and I found ourselves in a fascinating year-long course leading to a skipper's license for small craft. Diverse subjects were taught: sailing theory and practice, maritime map reading, radio communications, meteorology, diesel engines, first-aid, knots, and of course navigation, coastal and celestial. Surprisingly, at the Hilton beach, meanwhile, the construction of a marina had actually begun.

I did have a brush with sailing in my student days in Los Angeles. A kindly doctor acquaintance, Leonard Asher, who owned a sailboat and whose wife suffered from sea-sickness, had often invited me as deck-hand and nanny to his two children on weekend excursions to picturesque Catalina island, a half-day sail off the California coastline. It is there that the sailing bug had trapped me and lay dormant, waiting to come alive.

In those days, and perhaps today too, there was no international convention governing the requirements for skippers of small crafts. In Israel, partially surrounded by unfriendly countries, the requirements are quite rigorous, among other reasons, to prevent small boats from mistakenly entering inhospitable territorial waters.

After passing the government exams and obtaining the long awaited skipper's license, I committed to a splendid acquisition, a 9.30 meter long Yachting France fiberglass sloop, to be picked up in Hyeres, near Toulon. I went to the port authority in Haifa to register the boat. The registrar's name happened to be

Klemperer, and I could not help asking jokingly if by any chance the famous conductor Otto Klemperer was a relative. "Yes," Klemperer said, "my first cousin." Looking at my documents, he suddenly smiled, "Was my predecessor in this job, the maritime lawyer Julius Sebba, by any chance, *your* relative?" "Yes," I answered proudly, "not first cousin, but family." "And what is to be the name of your boat?" he inquired. "Does a boat need to have a name?" I asked. They did not teach us that in the course. "Yes, every boat has to have a name," he said, and waited for an answer. I had come to Haifa by train, and held in my hand a pocket edition of Stravinsky's *Firebird* Suite, which we were studying in class at the time. Almost without thinking, I said, "Firebird." Klemperer entered the name onto his forms. "Just a minute," objected Klemperer's middle-aged secretary," I think we *have* a Firebird." Klemperer doubted this, but the exacting lady brought out a heavy leather-bound book, the genuine boat register, and went through the entries several times. No boat by that name was to be found. "I am sure there was a Firebird," she insisted. I thought I might come to the lady's rescue. "Perhaps you are thinking of Stravinsky's *Firebird*," I suggested, waving my pocket score in her direction. "Oh, Stravinsky, yes, of course," she said, much relieved. "Tell me, perhaps you know, where does he keep it, in the Kishon river or in Jaffa?"

Sailing is one of mankind's oldest and most elemental advances, not unlike making a fire, or conceiving the wheel. Though constantly refined through the ages, sailing is essentially not much different today than it was five or ten thousand years ago. The wind is there anyway, and it carries the boat, without having to invest extra energy and deplete a vanishing resource. There is no sound, except the sliding of the hull through the water. No smell of gasoline or diesel, no vibration of any kind. Once the coastline disappears below the horizon, the hassle of civilization becomes but a vague reminiscence, and one becomes inescapably aware of being alone in the universe. In a way, one might as well be on the other side of the moon.

The maiden voyage of *Firebird* turned into one of the most enjoyable odysseys of my life. The new boat itself was perfection. The cabin was deep enough for a person to stand up comfortably, yet without the superstructure protruding too much above the deck to slow down the boat's progress. There were six bunks, all fitted out pleasingly with small reading lights—two in the bow, two along the central folding table, and a double bunk in the so-called 'Captain's Cabin,' which featured its own door, and in which I installed an extra compass near my head to make sure even in my sleep that the boat was sailing on course. There was also a galley with a small refrigerator, a navigation corner, which I furnished with a set of relevant British Admiralty maritime maps, a shower/toilet all in white, and plenty of storage space for gear and water.

From the little French port of Hyeres, manned by a crew of four, *Firebird* sailed through the Ligurian Sea to Ajaccio, Corsica, and on through the Strait of Bonifacio (between Corsica and Sardinia) via the Tirrhenian Sea to the Western Coast of Italy. A short stop at the island of Capri to re-supply and a switch to the second crew, and on south, through the Strait of Messina (between the Italian mainland and Sicily), Reggio di Calabria, across the Golfo di Taranto and the last bit of Italy, Santa Maria di Leuca. Crossing the Adriatic Sea through the Strait of Otranto, we sailed to the island of Corfu, Greece, and a meeting with the third crew. Cephalonia, in the Ionian Islands, the Corinthian Sea, and through the man-made Corinthian Canal into the

Saronic Gulf, the island of Hydra, the Cyclades and the island of Mykonos, where we met the fourth and last crew. From there we sailed east to the Dodecanese Islands, via charming little Symi, which became one of my favorites, then to Rhodos, and from there via Paphos in Cyprus, home to the Tel-Aviv Marina.

The four 'crews' were friends who flew out to meet me on pre-arranged dates for about two weeks each. The law does not require a crew member to have special qualifications, so anyone can come aboard as crew. However, teammates are expected to take turns, day or night, either at the tiller, keeping the boat on course, or as look-out at the bow, to avoid collision. A standing order I insisted upon during night sailing was to alert or wake me if a light was seen on the open sea. Ships have a clever illumination protocol, by which an observer can determine the vessel's size and direction. Although not too complicated even for a novice to learn (seeing a green and a red light simultaneously means the vessel is coming toward you), I felt it my duty to be around and avert the remotest chance of getting onto a collision course. As skipper, I never left the boat unless it was securely moored, and never slept 'out,' finding the captain's cabin the most luxurious accommodation imaginable.

Ever since that voyage I have always asked my guests to bring one outfit in white, for 'formal' occasions, such as reporting to the border police and customs when entering or leaving a country. In spite of limited space, the library shelf above the navigation table contained one item not connected to sailing: the four-voice chorales of J.S. Bach. These came in handy when waiting out a storm in a secluded haven, and in truth I favored, where possible, teammates who could read solfege. At the end of each trip abroad, there would be a joyous captain's dinner, when all leftover food was brought out and a fancy menu in French was composed and read out aloud.

There are two things a sailboat cannot do. One, much like a bicycle, it cannot be controlled at very low speeds. For this reason, sailboats are equipped with an auxiliary motor, usually a diesel engine, for navigating within a Marina or a harbor, and also for stabilizing the boat at sea in very bad weather. Two, a sailboat cannot sail into the wind, and if this is one's course the boat must zig-zag left and right to overcome the dead angle around the wind's direction. Generally, a boat under sail will be tilted to either left or right, so bunks, shelves, and surfaces have rims or frames around them. Especially when tacking, anything left loose or untied instantly flies off the deck, never to be seen again.

Unlike ships, characteristically equipped with powerful high-voltage radio transmitters, small boats communicate by radio on a so-called 'channel 16' wavelength. This compact, low-voltage device, however, has of necessity a limited range. A sailboat on its way from Israel to Cyprus—the nearest approachable destination—inevitably passes through a zone of 'radio silence,' too far out from *Haifa Radio*, and not yet close enough to *Akrotiri*, the Cypriot contact located high up in the Trodos mountains. In case of an emergency no one in the world would hear you, nor be able to offer assistance or advice. Habitually I forewarned my teammates to be doubly cautious on this stretch, until radio contact was re-established. In my sailing days, before mobile phones and GPS devices became household articles, this expanse was a yachtsman's unavoidable peril, yet at the same time an extraordinary thrill. One time we were caught in this section without wind at all. We could either start the engine, or wait for the westerly trade to build up again. We opted, in true yachtsmen's spirit, not to touch the engine, and spent two happy days cut off from the world.

The heart of navigation is, of course, establishing where on the endless waters you actually are. When land is visible, the solution is fairly simple. By measuring the compass bearing to two recognizable points which are represented on your map, you draw two corresponding lines from those points back out to sea, and where these two lines cross, known as a *fix*, that is your position.

With no land in sight, you are dependent on celestial bodies to guide you—the sun during the day, and the stars at night. Trouble is, sun and especially the planets behave somewhat irregularly, posing a serious brainteaser to the baffled human observer. All through antiquity it was assumed, and bitterly defended by the Church, that the center of the universe, around which all heavenly bodies circle, is the earth. Only in 1543 a Polish monk, Nicolaus Copernicus, suggested that the sun, not the earth, was the center of the universe, and that the earth, itself a planet, circled the sun. The Italian scientist Galileo Galilei, developer of the telescope, came to the same conclusion, and paid a high price for upholding this view, as dramatized by Bertolt Brecht in his famous play *Galileo*. In 1609, the German mathematician Johannes Kepler, in one of humanity's most striking deductions, formulated several rules which laid the foundation for modern science and astronomy. Kepler's first law states that the orbit of every planet is an ellipse with the sun at one of the two foci. His Second Law, even more spectacular, says that a line joining a planet and the sun sweeps out equal areas during equal intervals of *time*. I found these insights, which we learnt in the skipper's course, deeply compelling, and wonder to this day which is the greater marvel—the universe being constructed in such an orderly fashion, or the human mind capable of comprehending and uncovering this.

Once the position of a major heavenly body can be accurately predicted, it can be used as a reference point to determine the observer's location. All a navigator needs on board is a chronometer (showing Greenwich Mean Time), a sextant (a hand-held instrument measuring the vertical angle between sun or star and the horizon), and a current Almanac (published annually) listing the coordinates of the major bodies throughout the year.

"Sailing keeps the doctors away," a Turkish yachtsman once told me. Indeed, sailing is a healthy sport, and a few weeks on a boat can do wonders to one's constitution. A ten-liter jerry-can filled with water or fuel begins to feel lighter by the day. Sometimes there is a need to dive under water to inspect the hull from the outside, or to pull oneself upward on a trapeze to the top of the wildly swinging mast to replace a defunct light-bulb, obligatory for sailing at night. During my sailing days I met several families, some with children, who had given up living on land altogether. It is amazing how little living space and few earthly goods one really needs. I developed a tremendous respect for those who had actually braved the oceans for weeks without seeing land, crossing the Atlantic or the Pacific, and for whom the Mediterranean Sea was merely a gentle lake for wintering.

On Saturdays the Tel-Aviv Marina is a bustling meeting place. Visiting neighboring boats is a popular social activity, and there is always work to be done on one's own boat. One day a persuasive salesman came round with a small portable water purifier, an invaluable device no yachtsman could disregard. To demonstrate, the fellow invited a group of us to urinate into the device's container. We all consented and contributed our share. A few minutes' connection to the boat's battery, and *voila!* the liquid is purified. He filled a glass with it, now admittedly colorless, and to our incredulity drank the contents with an expression of great pleasure. The sell, however, was too hard. No one bought the contraption from him. One was rather left with the Ancient Mariner's agonizing words ringing in one's ears, 'Water, water, everywhere, and not a drop to drink' (Samuel Taylor Coleridge, 1798).

During thunderstorms in the winter months, especially at night, the Marina quickly springs to life. Yachtsmen forever worry that their (or their neighbors') boats will tear loose from their moorings and cause havoc. It is wise, therefore, to stick around and see that no harm befalls your boat. During a storm, it is said, a boat is safest out in the open sea, where there is, presumably, nothing to collide with. In such weather, however, fog and spray, strapping winds, and high waves can put this claim to the test. In a strong wind, I was always astonished how fast the boat moved with the main-sail trimmed down to the size of a mere handkerchief.

Greece, with its 4,000 islands, is one of the world's favorite destinations for recreational sailing. The dramatic island formations, the picturesque waterfront bays, the little stone houses and narrow alleys, perennially white-washed with wooden shutters and balustrades painted mostly in dark blue, are a photographer's paradise. Indeed, the photos I took on these islands over the years are among the best I ever did. Luckily only the major islands are overrun by tourists. For the independent yachtsman there are enough isolated islets left to visit and to savor the true local atmosphere. If there is a general store, yoghurt is still sold in home-made earthenware, and if there is a post office, and mail for you marked *poste restante*, the postmaster himself will bring the mail to your boat, and have time for an *arak* or a 'Greek' coffee in your cockpit. On reflection, one cannot escape the tantalizing speculation as to what precisely it was that caused the very foundations of Western culture, art, science, architecture, and philosophy to be born, of all places, on these islands.

Sailing can be full of surprises. Way out at sea, one encounters lone seagulls, overly brave or perhaps lost and almost exhausted. Occasionally playful dolphins swim along the boat for many nautical miles. Once we passed a huge sea turtle enjoying itself, unperturbed by our intrusion. Approaching Larnaca one evening after several days at sea, we were overwhelmed by the smell of tasty kebab wafting across the water, although we were still hours away from land. At the island of Castelorizo near the Turkish coast, after a long night's journey, we saw the most majestic sunrise, in full color and as if in slow motion.

When another sailboat approaches at sea, people happily wave to each other, as though the brotherhood of men has become a reality. One eagerly appraises the passing boat, its size, and especially its speed, and wonders where these travelers come from. Once we got the answer gratis. In a very British accent someone hollered across the waters, "Ahoy there."

Out at sea, suddenly a Navy vessel is alongside us, and we are ordered by megaphone to open Channel 16. It is the Israel Navy, and the conversation switches from English to Hebrew. A quick check to ascertain who we are, and all is found to be in order. The Navy vessel wishes us well, presses its accelerator harder than necessary so our boat shakes and shudders, and flies away.

Thinking back, those years presented a perfect way of life: summers on the boat, winters at the university; a balanced regimen of body and mind. My doctorate was approved, and I was given the opportunity to teach my findings. My conducting studies also began to bear fruit, and I became too busy to pursue all three endeavors. Although I hate to admit it, the sun actually became a bit too strong for me. My good friend Pinni (Pinchas Eshet), a well-known sculptor and art professor who had sailed with me often, obtained his skipper's license and bought my boat.

For a year or two I didn't run into Pinni. When we met again, I was sorry to learn that he had separated from his wife, left her their apartment, and had gone to live on the boat. Somewhat apologetically he added that he had also changed the boat's name. "Why did you do that?" I asked, although it was his perfect right to do so. "Well," he said, "every time the Navy caught me at sea, the story repeated itself. 'Who do you say you are? *Feierberg*? Sorry, there is no such name on the register.' I finally decided to simplify the procedure."

Keeping the boat on course

With fellow yachtsman Zubin Mehta

11

All the King's Men

Directing Edward G. Robinson in documentary Israel, Ancient Caesarea, 1959 (Rubinger)

In 1960 the Prime Minister's office decided to give the fledgling film industry in Israel a vital push, and invited an experienced Hollywood screenwriter to Israel, to give a serious creative course in screenwriting. The participants were to be the cream of the crop of Israel's authors, playwrights, publicists, commentators, and film people.

The person selected to lead the course was Chicago-born Carl Foreman, a superb choice. Foreman had written some of the most successful films of all time, among them *High Noon, The Bridge on the River Kwai,* and *The Guns of Navaronne.* He had worked with such top directors as Fred Zinneman and David Lean, often acting as producer and director himself, and he had garnered numerous Academy Awards and nominations for his work. But there was more to him: he was a man of exceptional integrity. Having been briefly in his youth a member of the Communist party, he was called, during the production of *High Noon* in 1951, to testify before the infamous House Committee on Un-American Activities in Washington DC, and asked to reveal names of Hollywood figures with supposedly leftist political leanings. Citing the Fifth Amendment, he declined to do so. As a result, he was declared an 'uncooperative witness,' and was blacklisted in Hollywood. Out of work, he was forced to leave the USA. Relocating to London, he continued to write screenplays which were channeled back to Hollywood under fake names. In the ensuing years in England he wrote and produced quite a number of successful films, and was elected president of the Writers Guild of Great Britain. A British Academy of Motion Picture Special Award was established in his name. He became a governor of the British Film Institute, and was awarded a CBE.

At the first meeting of the course in Tel-Aviv, the fellow sitting next to me was Moshe Rashkes. He was a lean and athletic young man, and his face had a friendly, smiling expression. Wounded in the War of Independence, he had lost the use of one arm, but he was conspicuously devoid of bitterness, and throughout the course could always find something positive to say when asked to criticize a fellow participant's work. Rashkes was founder and president of the IDF Disabled Veterans Organization, and the head of a modest sports facility for the disabled, which during the following five decades he managed to develop into an exemplary international institution of disabled sports. He belonged to the generation of Israel's young writers, as he had written a best-selling book in Hebrew on his experiences in the war, titled *Days of Lead* (free translation). We sat together during the entire course, and became close friends.

I was invited to the course, I assume, on the basis of my film studies in California, and perhaps especially because I had just directed a documentary film on Israel, made and widely distributed by Warner Bros in conjunction with the United Jewish Appeal. In this 40-minute film, the veteran actor Edward G. Robinson walked along Israel's varied locations, and after final editing, he narrated the film. The writer of the narration was the celebrated author of *Exodus*, Leon Uris, who came to Israel for the production. An enthusiastic admirer of the Israeli-born 'Sabra' type, whom he described as "a guy who can take a thick telephone book and tear it in half with his bare hands," Uris liked to play-act the Sabra type himself. Traveling by jeep to our various locations, dressed in short sleeves and khaki shorts, and driving the jeep himself, he was accompanied by a Foreign Office employee who had been assigned to him. The somewhat bashful fellow was always immaculately dressed in a dark-blue suit, with briefcase in hand, and Uris got a great kick every time a small crowd gathered round the vehicle, making a big fuss about the fellow in the suit, ignoring the 'driver' completely.

Foreman's course was a fascinating eye-opener for everyone and lasted several months. At the last session, Foreman suggested that we form an Israel Writers Guild, like the ones in Hollywood and London, to advance and protect the country's writers of film. Rashkes and I knew something like that might come up. I rose and said: "Mr. Foreman, I ask for your indulgence, this will take but a minute." Turning to the assembly, I said, "I call for an extraordinary meeting of the future Israel Writers Guild, and declare the meeting open. Is there a motion on the floor?" Rashkes responded on cue. "Yes. I move to elect Mr. Carl Foreman to the post of Honorary President of the Israel Writers Guild." "Is there a second?" I inquired. "I second," shouted someone we had organized to do so beforehand. "All those in favor please raise their hands." Without exception, everyone did so. "The motion is carried," I announced. "The extraordinary meeting is now adjourned. Mr. Foreman," I continued, "I am honored to inform you that you have just been unanimously elected Honorary President of the Israel Writers Guild. Congratulations." "Democracy at work," said a pleased Foreman. "I knew something was up, Sam, when I saw you come in tonight wearing a suit and tie for the first time."

Within a few months the Israel Writers Guild became a registered non-profit organization. I was elected president and Rashkes vice president, and soon afterwards came an invitation from the Writers Guild of Great Britain to come to London for a meeting intended to establish an International Writers Guild. I attended that meeting, and the Israel Writers Guild thus became one of the founding members of the international organization.

In the following years there were several International Writers Guild ("IWG") meetings—in Paris, Monte Carlo, and Varna, all of which, as Israel's delegate, I attended, some with Rashkes. It was exciting to meet so many creative minds from different parts of the world, and a great joy to meet again those who had been present on previous occasions. I became aware of the importance of Israel's participation in international events. It seemed also that the Israeli delegates were the persons to whom Jewish delegates came to identify themselves, particularly if their names or their looks were not typically Jewish. A tall well-built Canadian, in a moment alone, confided in passing, "In my youth I was in the *Hashomer Hatsa'Ir* movement." The East German delegate surprised me with a whispered "I have a sister in Israel." One of the Frenchmen commented jokingly, "I think the only ones who are definitely not Jewish are the two Japanese." In Paris I became friendly with the ageing Russian-Jewish film-maker Aleksei Kapler, whose short-lived romance long ago with Stalin's daughter Svetlana had cost him five years' imprisonment in Siberia. He was keen to know all he could about Israel. Having by now become an old hand at IWG issues, I was elected in Varna to the executive board of the organization.

In 1969 the big event of the IWG was its World Congress in Moscow, which both Rashkes and I were to attend. The Cold War, however, was still in full swing. The Soviet Union had severed diplomatic relations with Israel after the Six-Day War, two years earlier, and this enabled Moscow to be evasive about granting Rashkes and me entry visas to Russia. While our participation was still in question, I received a very polite call from our own Foreign Office cautioning us, in case we would be allowed to go, against engaging in intimate relations with Russian women, as that might be a trap. The warning was delivered in beautiful diplomatic lingo, as befits a Foreign Office. In the end it was due to the pressure from leading Western Writers Guilds, threatening to boycott the Congress if Israel were not there, that at 05:00 on the day of the delegates' arrival I got a wake-up call at home from a certain Mr. Karaganov in Moscow, informing me that visas would be waiting for us that day at the Soviet Embassy in Nicosia, Cyprus. Having prepared for this possibility, Rashkes and I hurriedly proceeded to the airport and were lucky to get to Cyprus before the Russian Embassy closed at noon. We were given the visas, but the only useful flight for us was one via Warsaw, and it was fully booked. Now the Israel Embassy in Nicosia came to our rescue. They managed to have two passengers taken off the flight, and we got on. Needless to say, Rashkes and I felt that we owed the Russians a suitable response to their somewhat inhospitable conduct.

I had in those days a second passport, which luckily I used for this trip. As soon as we arrived in Moscow, Rashkes' Israeli passport was taken from him, and he was led to a small room and told to wait. I went with him till I knew where he was being held, then hurried to the airport arrivals hall to see if perhaps some other delegates were there. Luckily I saw several, from the US and Britain, who had just arrived. Quickly I explained Rashkes' detention, and immediately they said they would not leave the airport without us. I rushed between Rashkes and the group repeatedly to keep in touch. Not one delegate agreed to take the waiting transport to the hotel. After several hours' deadlock, late into the night, Rashkes' passport was returned to him, and wild shouts of triumph welcomed him when he and I finally emerged as free men.

The assembly next morning was distinguished. Twenty countries had sent delegations. Present also were observers from UNESCO and several other international organizations, and a large group of local spectators, writers and intellectuals, who filled the gallery. The US delegation included such well-known names, and Writers Guild of America Presidents, as

Mel Shavelson (*Cast A Giant Shadow*, shot in Israel), Michael Blankfort (*The Caine Mutiny*), and Christopher Knopf (*Equal Justice*). From Writers Guild of America East came Ernest Kinoy and Manya Starr. Britain had sent IWG President Leigh Vance, David Whitaker and Alan Griffiths; France, Paul Vialar and Roger Fernay; West Germany, Dr. Alfred Unger; and Russia, our friend Aleksei Kapler, as head of the Russian delegation. The first session was devoted to each member country giving a report of their country's film activity since the last general assembly. When it came to Israel's turn, I explained that Rashkes had prepared the report, but because his English was practically non-existent (a blatant lie), would the chair permit him to speak Hebrew, and in case there was no Hebrew interpreter around (fat chance there would be), I would translate into English sentence by sentence. There was a chuckle of support and approval from many delegates, especially those who had waited at the airport the night before, and a stir of excitement in the gallery. The stratagem worked. Hebrew resounded at the session and earned a wave of applause.

Emboldened, a few days later on a Friday, as the afternoon session was declared open, I raised a point of order. The Sabbath nearing, I feared we would be late for prayer at the synagogue, and requested that our delegation be excused. Although in truth I had not been to synagogue since my Bar-Mitzvah, and the sunset in Moscow in July (signaling the Sabbath's entry) does not occur till the late hours of the evening, permission by the session's chair was granted. To our surprise, many other delegates decided to join us. At Moscow's Great Synagogue, all but empty, our group was greeted by Moscow's Chief Rabbi. "We know of your being in the country, and we welcome you. Please tell me which of you is Rashkes and which is Zebba."

It was the only outing we had without official chaperones in evidence.

Our activities at the Congress, however, were not limited to making mischief. We strongly supported a call for a resolution deploring the persecution of writers anywhere in the world, in which the Congress was split exactly along Cold War lines. On another occasion, using my German, I suggested to the East and West German delegations to sit together with me at dinner one evening, and it was the first time they spoke to each other.

When at the last session it came to the elections of officers, I was voted Vice President of the International body. It was more than I would ever have bargained for. I fulfilled my duties conscientiously for the next three years. Meanwhile, both Rashkes and I heaved a sigh of relief when our plane rose into the sky, leaving Moscow's Sheremetyevo International Airport behind.

12

The Sound Of Music

Honing my new trade (Rozanski)

It all started because of Shalom Ronly Riklis. "Come visit my conducting class at the Academy," he said to me, and added, "I know you are dying to conduct." I had known Prof. Riklis by sight, from concerts at the Israel Philharmonic, where he served as house conductor, and from the Rubin Music Academy at Tel Aviv University, where he taught; but I think it was the first time we had actually spoken. It was at the home of a mutual friend, during a small gathering to celebrate my completing the PhD, in 1980. I wondered what made him say that to me, especially his conclusion that I was "dying to conduct," something that had never entered my mind before. He was perhaps recruiting for his class, and he may have seen me occasionally turning pages for pianist Pnina Salzman. And yet, it was a sentence that changed my life. After one class, I was hooked.

For three years I attended Riklis' conducting class, participated as timpanist in the Academy Orchestra, studied orchestra scores, and watched IPO rehearsals with renowned conductors. The first thing we needed to learn, Riklis had instructed us from the beginning, was how to sneak into the Mann Auditorium without getting caught, and the second was to find a seat far enough and dark enough so that the stage manager shouldn't notice and throw us out. At this I became quite proficient, perhaps because I was at least twice the age of my classmates and a less suspicious-looking infiltrator into the Holy of Holies.

Riklis was a modest and dedicated person. Once, after a concert of the IPO he had conducted, I went backstage to congratulate him. "Listen," he said to me, "Don't conduct like I conduct. Conduct like I teach." Stunned by such frankness, I did not find the words to answer him. On another occasion there was a strike at the University and classes were cancelled for over a month. Riklis said the class could go on quietly off campus, and my apartment being close, I was glad to provide the classroom facility. I particularly remember the first time our class was to actually conduct the Academy Orchestra. This happened only once per semester, the orchestra having to serve the composition and the orchestration classes as well, in addition to its main function of learning to play orchestra repertoire. Each of us was allotted maybe ten minutes of orchestra time, with one guy watching the clock and calling out when one's time was up. We were all very excited, as evidenced by the steady traffic of our class members between the rehearsal hall and the men's room. Indeed, the sensation of moving one's arm and the whole orchestra suddenly coming in, is incredibly powerful. It is also incredibly precarious: if the orchestra does not begin together, it is the exclusive fault of the conductor. How true the old saying is: 'there is no such thing as a poor orchestra, only a poor conductor.'

Actually, I found out later, this statement is not entirely accurate. An orchestra also has a condition to fill: players must patently watch the conductor. New and inexperienced orchestra players will often shy away from lifting their eyes off the page, afraid perhaps of losing their place in the score, resulting thus in their guessing the entrance or relying on a neighbor to start playing. It becomes the conductor's responsibility to demand this aptitude adamantly from every orchestra player.

In those days I felt like a small boy with a new toy. Trouble was, except for waving my arms about at home to the sound of a record, something I had already done at age four, the chances of my ever standing in front of a live orchestra were about zero. A conductor, much like an airplane pilot, needs hundreds of hours of practice to hone his craft. A music academy is not built to provide this, and surely no one would offer us a job without experience, especially me, now in my later fifties. The only way, I deduced, was to have a practice orchestra of my own. Thus, with Riklis' blessings, the consent of our Dean Prof. Abraham Ronen, and the encouragement of University President Prof. Haim Ben-Shahar, I founded the Campus Orchestra, an amateur ensemble open to students, faculty, and others, and became its conductor and music director, if—that is—I could find the players to form the orchestra.

Clearly, a lot of intelligence was required to find prospective candidates. Once accosted, many tended to decline, some because they considered their standard too low to join an ensemble, others because they considered it too high. Some disliked the commotion and noise of an orchestra, others disliked the passivity required. Many were indisposed to making a commitment. Here and there a candidate was willing to join, but had no instrument. Of flautists, apparently the most popular of instruments, there were enough to fill half a dozen symphony orchestras, but oboists and bassoonists could not be found for love or money, and there were never enough lower strings, especially violas. I did not know then that an orchestra needed to own, or have at its disposal, heavy and expensive instruments such as double basses, timpani, various percussion, sometimes English horn, bass-clarinet, contra-bassoon, glockenspiel, celesta, and harp.

Previously, I had never noticed people with instrument cases walking in the streets. Now I spotted them all the time, and by the shape of their cases I knew what instrument they played. Often I approached such individuals. "Excuse me, are you a professional musician?" Sometimes the answer would be an embarrassed, "No, I am just an amateur player." "Good," I'd say, "I'd like to talk to you." One time while stopping my car at a red light, someone bumped into me from the back. We both inspected the slight damage and decided to exchange details for insurance. "Is this *music paper* you are writing on?" asked the man. "Yes, why do you ask?" "Oh, many years ago I played the viola in the Gadna Youth Orchestra." "In that case, forget the insurance details. The bump will cost you in a different way."

The fellow promptly became a first desker in my understaffed viola section. On another occasion I was deeply impressed by a Russian lady who played the violin on a street corner. Talking to her, she was willing to join our orchestra, but had an unusual condition: I must never divulge to her daughter, a music student at the Academy, that her mother was playing in the streets to help her through her studies. Needless to say, I honored that request conscientiously.

Quickly I learnt that in an amateur group, where players' commitment depends on nothing but personal enjoyment, an orchestra's survival is a shaky business. Without contract or obligation, if a player isn't totally satisfied, he won't be back, and any given rehearsal may be the orchestra's last. Once, in the early stages of our existence, this actually happened, but a handful of us persisted and we started again. Ever since, I considered it a near miracle when at the start of a rehearsal the orchestra was actually seated and ready.

From the start cardinal questions challenged me, many of them to this day. Am I clear in my movements, and do they properly express the musical text? Do I stop the orchestra too often, or perhaps not often enough? Do I diagnose weaknesses correctly and fast enough? Are my tempi acceptable, is my beat steady, are my *rubati* reasonable? Do I manage to bring about an improvement? Am I sufficiently compelling to unite everyone? Do I not bore the orchestra, or disturb its musical flow?

In 1982, in spite of the obstacles, and within the academic year of its founding, the Campus Orchestra performed its opening concert at the Bar-Shira Auditorium, then the University's biggest hall. I ascribed the large audience to two main factors: one, the participation of Germany's much-admired

Ambassador Niels Hansen, who had accepted my invitation to join the orchestra as first flautist. That could have explained the presence of so many distinguished guests and diplomats. Two, there was also a large contingent of my own buddies, who I suspect had come partly to see me making a grand old fool of myself in a public spectacle.

Despite my apprehensions, the concert passed quite well. Within a short time *Campus* grew to a body of eighty players, and I ran it for over twenty years. We covered a great deal of classical repertoire, played concerts all over the country and once even abroad, and presented a whole array of rising young soloists both from Israel and from abroad, including some well known soloists such as Boris Belkin, Isabelle Faust, and Maxim Vengerov.

Sadly, Riklis fell ill much too young, while at the peak of his career. I visited him in hospital. He was cheerful and looked well, and I fully believed him when he said he'd be home in a few days. He knew the truth, however, as I later found out, and within a day or two he died.

Feeling the need for more instruction, I spent many a summer attending master classes with eminent conductors in what may be called the 'conducting capitals' of the world: Salzburg, Vienna, Sienna, Hilversum, Flaine, Dubrovnik, Schleswig-Holstein, Bergen, Santiago de Compostela, Dartington, Aspen. Not listed are the courses I was barred from attending because of admission age limits I had passed by more than a generation. Teaching techniques varied markedly, and courses offered a diversity of approaches. Practice was either without instruments, or with a piano, two pianos, a string quartet, a chamber orchestra, or a full symphony orchestra. There was much to learn everywhere, yet in many instances I felt students were given too much freedom to find their own expression, and not enough input to detailed hand, and to some extent, body movement, the conductor's true skill. One man whose teaching addressed that aspect head on was the Italian conductor Aldo Ceccato, who demanded ultimate precision in our waving, as though actually playing an invisible instrument. Ceccato was a fervent disciple of the great conductor Sergiu Celibidache, and he quickly became my favorite teacher. I went back to him repeatedly, and with his elegance, humor, and Italian-style English I learnt more than anywhere else "what is doing the director of a symphony orchestra," Throughout the years I have maintained a friendly relation with him and his lovely wife Eliana, herself a daughter of the famed Italian conductor Victor de Sabata.

With the massive influx of immigrants into Israel from the former Soviet Union in the early '90s, I got to know two or three newly arrived musicians. It struck me that if there were enough of them, I could form an ensemble and try my hand at conducting professional musicians. I invited the few I had met to my house one afternoon, and suggested they bring their instruments. Six or seven string players arrived, and I proposed that they consider forming a small ensemble, adding that I would be happy to work with them, but that my experience so far had been only with amateurs. This became an audition in reverse, the first time I stood before a group of professionals. We played a Mozart Divertimento, and the test was a revelation to me. Except for the upbeat (the entrance signal), I felt they didn't need me at all. At the end, to my delight, they asked to come back a week later, and this time a good fifteen players arrived. Two ladies were from the same orchestra in Kiev, and fell tearfully into each other's arms. Neither had told the other, nor anyone else, of their planned *Aliya* to Israel, to avoid complications with the authorities, and each of them, one day, had simply vanished. One young woman arrived with a violin in one hand and a baby on the other. The baby soon started to cry, screaming inconsolably. I ran down to neighbors I didn't actually know, but who had a baby, and the young mother came upstairs with Materna and baby bottles. Very soon the baby was quiet and we were able to resume playing.

The third time we met, no less than thirty musicians arrived, and as soon as the session ended I hurried down to the newly opened community center in our neighborhood, to ask for help. The young man in charge, Reiness was his name, heard me out and said okay, he'd write to the municipality and ask for permission to have our rehearsals there. "There should be an answer within two months," he added. "But I need a place next week," I said. Reiness thought for a moment and said, "I'll write the letter. Meanwhile, bring the orchestra." Without giving up *Campus*, my flagship, I started my second orchestra.

Some of the kind neighborhood ladies who brought home-cooked refreshments to the rehearsals were members of WIZO, the Women's International Zionist Organization, and word of our 'secret' activity at the community center reached the upper echelons of the organization. It did not take long for Wizo World President Raya Jaglom, one of the country's supreme fundraisers, to recruit the first two donors who enabled us to pay a modest remuneration to the players during their absorption period. The group thus became the Wizo Symphony Orchestra, by far the largest musical body in the country, and the fastest growing one, many of its players having heard of its existence already before their immigration. A good proportion of these excellent musicians eventually joined the ranks of the Israel Philharmonic and other distinguished orchestras.

I remember a particularly festive concert we played at the Hilton Hotel Ballroom to introduce the orchestra at an International Wizo Convention. We played Tchaikovsky's *Romeo and Juliet* to an excited crowd of delegates. Mrs. Jaglom was known for her uncanny knack of bestowing upon donors irresistible titles. Thus, a certain Mrs. Clara Sznajderman of Caracas, Venezuela, was the Orchestra's 'Honorary President,' and the Orchestra's by-line, 'In Memory of Herman Gertler,' was a fitting tribute to donor Moritz Gertler of Frankfurt, Germany. Herman Gertler, Moritz's young brother, had been a gifted young violinist who perished in the Holocaust in Poland. We had just finished our performance and Moritz Gertler came up to me in a somber emotional mood. Before he managed to speak to me, Mrs. Sznajderman suddenly approached us, waving her program in the air. "Look, what is this Gertler thing in the program? Who is this Gertler anyway?" she demanded in a heavy East European accent. The end of our funding has arrived, I concluded, and said sweetly, "Oh, Mrs. Sznajderman, this is Mr. Gertler, our other donor. Since he may not speak Spanish, and you perhaps do not speak German, maybe you both speak Polish?" The chance I took paid off. They were both originally from Poland, spoke Polish fluently, and remained inseparable for the rest of the evening.

About that time I received my first invitation as guest conductor abroad. It was from the *Orquesta Sinfonica Nacional de El Salvador,* a spirited ensemble of young players, and it started me on a new and exciting chapter: *Have baton, will travel.*

On the night of the concert in San Salvador, attended by El

Salvador's President Alfredo Cristiani, Israel's Ambassador David Cohen at his side in the Presidential Box, I was just ready to step onto the stage when a young man speaking Hebrew approached me. As Israel Embassy's security officer, he explained that in the aftermath of the long civil war (1980–1992) that had just ended, *if* there should be a shooting incident–a conductor's back being a convenient target–and *if* I should get hurt and be carried off the stage *without* losing consciousness, and *if* among those carrying me would be a fellow in a blue blazer, it would mean I was not being kidnapped, the blazer fellow being one of our men, and he would be standing throughout the concert on the right side of the auditorium. Fine, I noted, in that case, nothing to worry about, and stepped onto the stage. Aware of being on the wrong end of a possible target practice, I was eager to locate the blue blazer before the shooting, or the music, began. While graciously acknowledging the welcoming applause, I carefully scanned the auditorium's right side, but found no one to answer the man's description.

The concert opened with Beethoven's *Coriolan* Overture. Normally there is little excuse for a conductor to turn much to his right, where the celli and basses are, but luckily the *Coriolan* ends with a long quiet passage of celli basses. All through the overture I turned often to the violins on my left, so that toward the end I would be justified in turning to the right. And as the music came to its sad and subdued end, halleluya, out of the corner of my eye I suddenly spotted the blazer, and felt much safer for the rest of the evening.

Toward the end of Niels Hansen's assignment in Israel, the President of the Federal Republic of Germany, Richard von Weizsäcker, came on an official visit to Israel. At a reception in his honor, Hansen introduced me to the President, to whom

I related Hansen's much appreciated music activity with the Campus Orchestra, adding how sorry we were to lose such a good friend. "No," Weizsäcker corrected me, "you are not losing a friend, only his presence."

When his post in Israel was over, Ambassador Hansen was appointed Germany's Ambassador to NATO, the second most prestigious diplomatic post after Washington DC. At that time I was invited to conduct the Phillips University Orchestra in Marburg, Germany. I wrote to Ambassador Hansen and asked if he would consider playing Mozart's *Andante for Flute*, a well-known short piece for flute solo and orchestra. He agreed willingly. There was a minor question of how best to get him from Brussels to Marburg for one evening. Driving was too cumbersome, and flying, via Frankfurt, too time consuming. The solution finally reached was elegant. A NATO military helicopter landed at an American Army base near Marburg, and out stepped Germany's Ambassador with a flute in his hand. It was surely one of NATO's most endearing peace missions ever undertaken.

As guest conductor one gets to see the world. Omsk, in Siberia, was closed to the world during Soviet days because of its military industries, and even now, ten years after Perestroika, it remained isolated and devoid of global advances. The Omsk Philharmonic Orchestra was made up of good musicians, most of them graduates of the famous music conservatory in Novosibirsk, but it was too poor to purchase published orchestra material from abroad. A copyist was constantly at work producing hand written parts for the players. Even photocopy machines were not available. The orchestra's timpani, built of copper kettles, looked like pock-marked planets bombarded by asteroids for millions of years.

In Buenos Aires I was introduced to the music of Argentine composer Alberto Ginastera, and we performed his *Impressiones de la Puna*, for flute solo and orchestra. The piece is based on Indian melodies from the Puna region, and strongly reminded me of the melodies I had heard among Indians in Brazil while making *Uirapuru*. Years later I performed this piece in Israel with the Emeritus Chamber Orchestra and Tessa as soloist.

By far the wealthiest and most Western oriented country I visited was South Korea, where I was asked to do a program in the Seoul Symphony Hall of three Mozart concerti—for one piano, two pianos, and three pianos, with six young Korean female soloists. I remember starting the first rehearsal with the concerto for one piano. A Steinway grand, the longest model, was rolled on to the stage. As I started the *tutti* (the orchestral introduction before the solo entrance), I turned to the young lady at the piano, "How's the tempo? Would you like it faster? Slower?" Ever so polite, she answered courteously, "Yes." After the concerto was over, stage hands rolled another Steinway grand to the stage, same model, and then a third one, same model again. It was a sight of affluence I had never seen before. After the concert performance, all six girls came to me, shy and giggling, covering their mouths with the palms of their hands, and presented me with a lovely traditional Korean landscape print, which ever since adorns our living room at home.

In Quito, Ecuador, I experienced one of nature's ugly phenomena, a volcanic eruption of the Pichincha, the nearby volcano, presenting an amazing view of a white mushroom cloud rising high into the sky, and a layer of ash covering the city. This happened on the day of my concert with the *Orquesta Sinfonica Nacional del Ecuador*, which did take place, but was naturally poorly attended. In truth, I felt we were under-rehearsed, the orchestra maintaining a schedule of changing programs every week, affording only four or five rehearsals per program. Meanwhile the airport was closed and I was stuck in Quito until further notice. In speaking to some of the players, they expressed frustration at being thus perpetually forced into mediocrity. By coincidence there was no program scheduled for the coming week, and it was a rare opportunity to try out a two-week rehearsal period for one program. Our extra concert, with everyone pitching in, became a notable success.

A very special engagement for me was with the Liepaja Symphony Orchestra in Latvia. Liepaja, the second largest city after Riga, was where my grandmother and most of the family had lived, and where as a child I was taken yearly by my mother to spend Passover. The orchestra thoughtfully suggested that I do Bruch's *Kol Nidrei,* and other works in this vein, but I could not bring myself to perpetuate the image of the persecuted diaspora Jew. Instead I asked to do a Chopin Piano Concerto with a spirited young Israeli soloist, Nadia Weintraub, and Brahms' Symphony No. 3, a work ending in somber universal anguish. My request was accepted without reserve.

All this came about thanks to Riklis' throwaway remark. Or did he know me better than I knew myself?

The Campus Orchestra (TAU)

The WIZO Symphony Orchestra (Rozanski)

With Campus concertmaster Eran Bourla moments before a concert (Rozanski)

German Ambassador and enthusiastic flautist Dr. Niels Hansen with harpist Ruth Bessman in Bizet's Carmen Suite (Rozanski)

Piano student (now Professor of Music) Dr. Asaf Zohar displaying ultimate calm and concentration (Rozanski)

*Revital Hachamoff playing
Chopin Piano Concerto No. 2
(Rozanski)*

*German violinist Isabelle Faust playing the Brahms Concerto
(Rozanski)*

With Maxim Vengerov after our performance (Rozanski)

Welcoming Halina Rodzinski (Rozanski)

With (from left) British Ambassador to Israel Sir Patrick Moberly,
Halina Rodzinski, and Lady Moberly (Rozanski)

13

Moments With Lenny

Leonard Bernstein didn't know me from Adam. Quite asymmetrically, I had known him for the better part of my life. Not actually known him personally, of course, but as for hundreds or perhaps thousands of my generation who had never or hardly ever met him, he was my private hero, my ultimate guru, the shaping influence of my musical life. Put on a Brahms symphony, any recording, and if Bernstein is conducting, I can identify him within the first three bars.

Bernstein entered my life when he was barely thirty, playing and conducting Beethoven's First Piano Concerto with the Los Angeles Philharmonic. It was a feat I had never seen before, nor had thought possible for any one person to accomplish. From then on I followed his concerts wherever I could, read his delightful and instructive books, watched his inimitable Young People's Concerts, pondered his uniquely annotated scores where available, and contemplated his celebrated Harvard University Norton Lectures. Luckily, living in Israel, there was no scarcity of his appearances throughout the years with the Israel Philharmonic, of which he was Laureate Conductor from 1947 until his death in 1990. He came to Israel often, in times of war or peace, and his presence instilled confidence in trying days.

I gained a closer glimpse of Bernstein at a one-day workshop for young conductors he gave at the Jerusalem Music Center around 1985. Two things about him amazed me. The first, after a whole day of intensive work, he continued the class, oblivious of the clock and to everyone's delight, for a good two hours after it was scheduled to end, so engrossed was he in his teaching. The second was his way of getting the participating chamber orchestra, the Israel Sinfonietta Beer Sheva, to pay closer attention to what the young conductors were doing. The orchestra, intimidated perhaps by the presence of the great Maestro, tended to play better than was called for by the students' gestures. To thwart this, Bernstein jumped onto the podium and instructed the orchestra to improvise anything that sprang to mind, provided it reflected *his* conducting. He gave an upbeat, and the orchestra responded. Bernstein was in turn happy, sad, angry, elated, slow, fast, addressing tutti, leading solos. The result was a breathtaking contemporary piece, a once-in-a-lifetime unwritten Bernstein opus. At once, a new bond formed between Bernstein and the Sinfonietta players, and needless to say, from then on the orchestra played exactly in accordance with the young conductors' indications, mistakes and all, imbuing the workshop with a rare and fascinating effectiveness.

Several years later I was actually introduced to Bernstein, briefly. He was due to arrive in Israel for a series of concerts with the Israel Philharmonic. This coincided with a private visit to Israel of a dear friend, Halina Rodzinski, widow of the famed conductor Artur Rodzinski. Halina, whom I had met in Rome more than twenty years earlier, was staying at my house, and was keen to say hello to Bernstein, as it was her husband, who as Music Director of the New York Philharmonic Orchestra at the time, had instructed his then unknown young assistant Leonard Bernstein to replace the ailing Bruno Walter the next evening–an event that became history. Halina was also well-known for the autobiographical book she had written about her life with her husband (*Our Two Lives,* Scribner's, New York, 1976).

When Bernstein's plane landed at Ben-Gurion, a signal went out to all IPO members, who were on alert, to assemble on stage for a rehearsal. That was the way Bernstein worked: no jet-lag for him. When the call reached me, for which I shall remain eternally grateful to the IPO telephonist, Halina the octogenarian was in my kitchen snipping the hair of two young sisters, Sinaya and Hefzibah Zer-Aviv, music students at Tel-Aviv University's Rubin Academy, who played in the Campus Orchestra, and whose hairstyles Halina had undertaken to improve. "Come immediately," the message said, "Maestro is on his way." "Let's take the girls with us," Halina suggested, and off we raced to the stage of the Frederic Mann Auditorium.

"What are you doing in Israel?" Bernstein cried out in astonishment when he saw Halina, the orthodox Catholic who had never been to the Holy Land before, and in front of the tuned and waiting orchestra he exuberantly greeted the elegant doyenne, including her entourage of the two sisters and me. Bernstein was clearly impressed by the exotic-looking girls, who indeed were a unique blend being half Tunisian and half Yemenite. "If all your orchestra looks like this," he mused, turning to me, "it doesn't really matter how well they play." He couldn't have chosen a more fitting compliment for the thrilled girls.

A few days later, at the Philharmonic guest house where Bernstein was staying, I received another invitation to be introduced to the Maestro. This time it came from my neighbor and acquaintance Enrice Barenboim, Daniel's father, to whom I had related the incident with Mrs. Rodzinski and the girls. "Look here," the expansive Barenboim challenged Bernstein when we met, "did you say that if the girls look pretty, it doesn't matter how they play?" I don't think Bernstein was particularly pleased with the question. "No," he retorted, "I said that..." He paused. "I probably said..." He paused again, "I hope I said..." And finally, "I *should* have said... that if they played the way they look, it would surely be a first-class orchestra." Never have I witnessed such a mix of candor, honesty, wit, and humor.

The last time I saw Bernstein was in Salzau, a sprawling country estate, where Bernstein conducted a week-long international orchestra workshop as part of the Schleswig-Holstein Music Festival. Closely encircled by helpers, camera crews, students, journalists, and signature seekers, Bernstein moved in and out of the enormous wooden rehearsal shed like a head of state. His sessions, notably those of Stravinsky's monumental *Le sacre du printemps,* were unforgettable. Considered undoable by a student orchestra, Bernstein explained, joked, demanded, sang, groaned, and aped "munching dinosaurs" until he achieved an inspired rendition of the piece rarely experienced anywhere before or since. Perhaps this was his true and fundamental calling—being an educator. Among the young, the aging Bernstein was young himself. At the end of each session he would leave the elevated stage, to everyone's momentary horror, by jumping down to ground level unaided, some five or six steps below. Miraculously, he remained unharmed.

As the last session ended, Bernstein suddenly noticed me

in the vast audience of auditors. "What are you doing here?" he yelled at me across the shed. The entire action around him stopped, and all eyes turned to me. Did he remember where he had seen me? There wasn't much time to formulate an answer. "I bring you regards from half of Israel," I yelled back. All eyes now turned to him, like at a tennis match. "Only half?" he hollered at me, "what about the other half?" This one was even harder to counter. "The other half," I screamed back, "didn't know I was coming here." For a moment I feared I had been too disrespectful, but Bernstein seemed pleased with our exchange. He laughed, waved a good-natured goodbye in my direction, threw his signature black cape with red silk lining around his shoulders and, followed closely by his many admirers, started out of the shed to the waiting limousine.

14

An Evening with Saleem

Young Saleem in Nazareth, circa 1990 *(Duaibis Abboud-Ashkar)*

Spring 1988. Saleem Abboud, aged eleven, became a celebrity in Israel. He was seen on prime time television playing the piano, that singular boy from around Nazareth who played Chopin. I did not see the program, but many of my friends told me about it, so I decided to look him up. He might be suitable for an appearance with our Campus Orchestra. I called the television authority. "What was his name?" they inquired. "When was he broadcast, on what program?" I didn't know. So how could they possibly help, "Don't we have enough pianists in Israel, even young ones?" "Hold on," I said, "this boy was special: he was Arab." "Ah, that's different," they said, they had all heard of him. Within a day I had his phone number.

His parents seemed pleased with my call. They invited me to come to their home in Nazareth to hear him. I said fine, but on second thought I consulted some friends who knew about security matters. In the territories dissent had been fomenting for weeks, and although well within the Green Line, Nazareth was Israel's largest all-Arab town. "Now," they said censoriously, "now you need to go, can't it wait?" I didn't follow their advice, and called to ask when I could come. "Not this week," they said, "the boy is to compete in a few days at the Clairmont Competition at Tel-Aviv University," three minutes from my home.

I was surprised. Clairmont is perhaps the toughest competition in the country, only the very best get to enter it. Would I come to hear him at the contest? He would be playing first in the morning, being the youngest. Impulsively, I invited them to come the day before and spend the night at my house. They said they'd think it over, and the next day called to say they would come. I quickly got organized for the visit.

Next evening at the allotted hour the doorbell rang. It struck me that this would be my first encounter with an Arab family. Absurd, in a way, over fifty years in the country, and how many Arabs did I know? When I was Saleem's age, during the mandate, I remember my parents having a number of Arab acquaintances, business connections, I think. Later, in my student days in California, while pitted against an Iraqi girl for the presidency of the foreign students' association, I opted for vice president and we won on the same ticket. Some years ago, on my sailboat at the Larnaca marina, my crew and I hosted a friendly honeymooning couple, which turned out to be from Kuwait. More recently, I befriended two Arab students, Taiseer Elias of the Hebrew University and Nizaar Raduan of the Haifa Technion, both of whom played the violin. We met at my house several times in preparation for their solo appearance with our orchestra in the Bach Double Concerto, and once I visited them in Taiseer's village of Shfar'am. That, more or less, was the extent of my knowledge of our neighbors.

Expectantly I opened the door, and my guests entered. Saleem was a handsome boy, tall for his age, with dark, penetrating eyes and long, soft hair. Maha, his mother, a petite and vivacious woman, exuded charm and goodwill from the start. And Duaibis, the father, was a tall, athletic figure, reserved and dignified. Nabeel, Saleem's younger brother who was also to come, was left with his grandmother in Nazareth.

Our meeting was easy and congenial. Maha had brought *labbane*, homemade, and *burma* and *pitta*. We had tea and snacks, and got acquainted. The Abbouds spoke fluent Hebrew, yet I preferred English: it seemed more neutral and appropriate. Duaibis was an electronics engineer, a Haifa Technion graduate. Maha was a therapist for deaf children, and had studied in France. They were Nazarenes both, for many generations. They lived in the big family house, one of Nazareth's oldest. Maha's brothers and sisters, even parents, had left Israel for San Diego and Florida, but Duaibis and Maha liked this country and stayed. We talked about many things—music, trips abroad, how their two children's characters differed, and how, by complete happenstance, they had acquired their piano, a Russian upright, in settlement of some transaction with a new immigrant, who wanted to exchange his piano for a car from the dealership where Maha temporarily worked, before Saleem was born. Before going to bed I watched Saleem as he slept, a fine face, framed in Paganini-like hair. We threw a small woolen blanket over his feet, one hand-knitted by my late mother.

In my room, I did not fall asleep for a while, reflecting on the ambivalence of human nature, on man's genius and folly, on his universality and his fatal tribalism. I wished Saleem well for tomorrow. I wished the other contestants well too. Three of the others that morning I knew well: they had already appeared with our orchestra as soloists—Yael Weiss, Ohad Ben-Ari, and Shlomi Shem-Tov, all exceptionally strong. How lucky I didn't have to be on the jury, I thought. I hoped my guests were comfortable. I heard them use the bathroom ever so quietly.

My musical meeting with Saleem came in the morning. I woke up to the sounds of Bartok's *For Children*. It never ceased to amaze me how the very gifted youngsters would not allow a wrong note or a poor phrase to pass by uncorrected. One would expect that of an adult, naturally, but in a child this is always astonishing. Yet in this lies the key to artistic advance: the constant watch, the critical ear, the endless patience, the perseverance to repeat a phrase a hundred times if necessary, until it becomes exactly what you want it to be, not an iota less. Perhaps competitions should be run this way, eavesdropping on a contestant practicing. One would immediately know whether the contender is merely a teacher's shadow, or an artist of promise. Saleem, unmistakably, belonged to the latter.

I showered hurriedly to join the young pianist. He was now working on Haydn's Sonata in E-flat Major, rendering it a clear,

articulate reading. From the bathroom I could hear, in addition
to the piano, a high-pitched human voice singing. That intrigued
me. We all know musicians who breathe loudly or emit all manner
of sounds while playing. Though devastating in performance
or in recording, while practicing it may not hurt to let oneself
be guided by intuitive singing. When I emerged into the living
room I discovered it was not Saleem singing, but Maha. It was
she who guided her son in the minute nuances of phrase and
dynamics. Aha, I realized, so there is an accomplished musician
in the family—no gift like this develops by itself. No, she said, she
had never studied music. She had wanted to very much as a girl,
but her father was against it, as it would be unfitting for a girl
to play an instrument. Maha did not use one word of musical
terminology, and did not as much as glance at Saleem's music,
yet her phrasing was faultless.

Maha asked what I thought of Saleem's playing. I doubted
if one should voice one's opinion an hour before a contest, and
I really thought he played excellently, but I did venture one or
two comments. I thought his pedaling could be a trifle cleaner,
and in the Haydn his beat could be just a little more accurate. I
even switched on the metronome, one of those newer devices
with a blinking red light Saleem had never seen before. He took
to it immediately, and in three minutes changed what might
take others months to accomplish. Significantly, at the contest
he remembered and stuck to his new ways.

We had breakfast and then set out. Saleem was not stressed,
nor were his parents. He still had half an hour left to be with
his teacher, Valeria Bruskin, who had just arrived from Haifa,
where she lived and taught. A new immigrant from Russia, she
had recently completed her Master's degree at the University's

Rubin Academy of Music, the very venue where the contest was now taking place.

Then Saleem opened the competition. The house was packed. At a long table facing the stage sat six jurors, four from Israel and two from abroad. Behind them, and extending out to the sides, many of them standing, were familiar faces from all over the country—teachers, music lovers, parents, even some very young yet attentive children, perhaps would-be contestants in years to come. When his name was called, Saleem went up to the stage confidently. He was dressed in a smart blue training-like outfit, and his long hair gave him an air of distinction. Deliberately he adjusted the height of his seat. Then, ready to start, he waited for complete silence. I know those moments well. There is a kind of mysticism in the air, transforming a hundred or a thousand states of mind into a single unified concentration. A hair too soon and you have not achieved it. A hair too late, and you have missed it. Saleem hit it precisely, and the piano responded. Music filled the hall, and reached into the hearts. It was clear that it was Saleem playing, not his teacher, not even Maha. When he finished, the applause was rousing, and he, typical of a fellow with integrity, was not satisfied with his performance.

As it turned out, Saleem did not win the competition. He was too young and inexperienced, and the other contestants, up to age seventeen in his class, were considerably older. It was actually the phenomenal Shem-Tov who won, for the third year in succession. But there could be no doubt as to Saleem's ability and flair, and my choice of him as a young soloist for next season was not difficult to make at all.

And so we parted. I would be going to Nazareth soon to visit my new friends. Maha promised the best Arab meal, and Valeria would soon decide which concerto Saleem should prepare for us, his first to be performed with orchestra.

Spring 1989. A year had gone by, and although the dissension, thought at first to have been but a temporary wave of unrest, had intensified into what became known the world over as the *Intifadah*, my friendship with the Abbouds flourished. The magnificent old stone house, built by Saleem's great-grandfather high on the mountainside overlooking the whole of ancient Nazareth, had become my second home. I was a weekend guest there countless times, and some of my friends were also allowed to share this privilege. Unforgettable were the cool moonlit summer evenings spent on the Abboud's imposing terrace, with its breathtaking view of the sacrosanct biblical town. Maha would serve goat cheese with grapes and pomegranates from the garden, and our conversation would be punctuated from afar by the ringing of church bells and the muezzins' calls for prayer.

On several occasions Saleem spent his school holidays with me in Tel-Aviv, and I must admit I felt immensely proud that his parents entrusted him to me. Now almost twelve, Saleem proved to be a most enjoyable companion. Together we listened to famous recordings, exercised intervals, charted the cycle of fifths, and identified chords. We went to hear piano recitals, attended the Israel Philharmonic Orchestra, and visited the Music Academy library. We met other young musicians, went shopping and swimming and, of course, worked on the concerto. Only once did he give me a scare. At a hamburger joint in our neighborhood, he announced gravely, "I am not coming to you anymore. You spend too much money on me." On another occasion, buying a metronome for him before going home, he insisted on participating in the purchase with a few coins he had in his pocket.

Valeria had decided that Saleem should play the celebrated Mozart D-minor Concerto, K. 466, a fine choice, though no easy assignment for a twelve-year-old. At first I was not overjoyed with this selection, fearing the magnitude and popularity of the work. Also, we had only recently done it with Yael Weiss, Saleem's Clairmont competitor four years his senior. This concerto, however, had traditionally been the first major vehicle for many a young performer, and it was assumed that its minor key and its oriental-sounding opening melody would make it particularly suitable for Saleem. We met regularly throughout the year, and to my great joy, I could see the concerto grow in Saleem's hands and take shape. It was not unusual for him to work four or five hours at a stretch without losing concentration, and his grasp of the work's structure and intricacy deepened from month to month. I was in awe not only of Saleem's own evolution, but also of Valeria's manifest eminence as a teacher. However, to avoid the risk of arousing Valeria's opposition to what might be construed as interfering in her work, we decided not to tell her too much of our meetings. This added to our alliance a special bond of secrecy. And so, as if this singular comradeship between a Jew and an Arab, between a man and a boy, were not incongruous enough, when it came to Mozart we were verily like thieves in the night.

For Saleem the year had been a good one. He grew in height and won a swimming championship in Nazareth. He excelled in math and biology and was selected to attend a youth week at the Weizmann Institute of Science in Rehovot. He won his third America-Israel Cultural Foundation scholarship in a row, with distinction. He played at the home of the French Ambassador to Israel, and was rewarded by a wealthy dowager's pledge of a grand piano for his school, the St. Joseph Seminary in Nazareth. He attended his first master class with a visiting artist at the notable Jerusalem Music Center. He was offered a scholarship for a music camp in Europe in the summer. He was summoned to meet and play for America-Israel Cultural Foundation President Isaac Stern. He was invited again to enter the Clairmont Competition, and this time he won First Prize.

Our orchestra rehearsals with Saleem started one week after the Clairmont. Although Saleem knew the concerto well by now, our common task was not always easy. The long and tiring drives from Nazareth, Saleem's hitherto limited exposure to ensemble playing, the poor quality, perhaps, of our rehearsal grand, did not enhance our work, and Saleem was clearly discontented with his playing. "I will kill him," a dissatisfied Maha said of her son, "I will go on the stage and kill him." Valeria, who was present, jumped up onto the stage and sat beside Saleem briefly. Instantly Saleem regained his composure and played on splendidly.

As luck would have it, we had to forgo a final rehearsal with Saleem just days before our gala, because of the Clairmont Awards Ceremony, in which he, as winner, was obliged to play. In lieu of that, I went to Nazareth the next day. We placed his upright and my conducting stand in the room's center, simulating a stage situation and, singing and shouting all the *tuttis,* went through the concerto thoroughly with an imaginary orchestra. That was probably the most useful of all our rehearsals. Saleem was now at ease with the interplay between soloist and orchestra, and we managed to maintain a vivid eye contact whenever needed to keep our beats synchronized.

Our first concert took place at Tel-Aviv's newly erected,

spacious Duhl Auditorium. Saleem wore a white silk shirt and black trousers, and looked elegant. He managed those last terrifying moments, waiting in the wings before stepping out, with poise and aplomb. Then the house lights dimmed, and there was silence. Saleem was greeted with an ovation the moment he set foot on the stage. Clearly the applause was directed at this striking, intense child, walking proudly to his place. Yet also, I am certain, it expressed a longing, a hope for a state of affairs far removed from the realities of our days. When the applause eventually subsided, I think all of us on the stage realized that we now had to make good on our symbolic promise.

The opening *tutti*, tricky at times because of its sustained syncopation, went well. There was drama in the highlights, delicacy in the wind-announced second theme, and tranquility in the soft remission towards the solo entrance. Saleem's opening came out just right. The enchanting melody, so Mediterranean in its minor key and ornamentation, might well have been invented in the stony, sweltering hills of the Galilee, rather than in the green, luscious slopes of Salzburg. Maha, with her unerring intuition, had often said that the entire concerto would depend on how those eight solo bars would be played, and so it was. Saleem gave them an introverted, sensitive interpretation, calm yet intense, controlled yet filled with emotion. From there the music took hold, just as Maha had predicted. Saleem was engrossed in his playing, and the orchestra members were alert, helpful, and anticipating. Saleem's cadenza was stunning, and the orchestral quiet homerun gentle and soothing. The second movement showed Saleem's lyrical qualities, his singing ability, his breathing. In the Intermezzo the woodwinds kept perfect pace with his pearl-like triplets. The solo announcement of the Finale, so typical of Mozart, was in good tempo, and the complex *tutti* following it, a virtuoso orchestral essay, exploded with joy.

Then it happened. Saleem's second solo, a virtual paraphrase of those famous eight opening bars, got stuck. The left hand, instead of following the right into the subdominant, stayed in the tonic. The dissonance sent ripples of panic into the house. Saleem's entire body writhed in pain as he struggled to regain his place. For a split second I thought of throwing my score onto the piano, or calling out a new letter. Had this happened while the orchestra played, he would surely have caught on, but now, with the orchestra silent and petrified, it was useless to go on. I gently motioned Saleem to stop, and asked if he would prefer to start the movement again. Yes, he nodded. Would he like to have the music, or at least to see my score? No, he shook his head. So we started again.

There was, of course, tremendous risk in this. What if he got stuck again at the same place? That would not only ruin our concert, it might have a devastating effect on his character and on his future. I could have, naturally, insisted that he keep the music on the piano, but for Saleem, that would have been outright humiliation. So, pretending to smile, I motioned Saleem to begin. His opening solo was fine. Our complex *tutti* was fine too. And now came Saleem's treacherous solo. He must have sensed that the entire house wished him good luck. We all held our breath. Saleem went through it beautifully without impediment, and when the orchestra took over we were visibly celebrating. I winked at him, and he acknowledged with a shadow of a smile. The rest of the movement was sheer delight. The gay oboe melody, even the subtle flute and bassoon dialogue, were all merriment. And the coda, in major key, with trumpets and timpani joining the fray, could not have been more appropriate to our spirits and our pride.

This time the applause for Saleem was rousing and, I dare say, doubly deserved, for his courage no less than for his artistry. Again and again he was called back to the stage, and he acknowledged the acclamation with a delicate Couperin encore, which exonerated him completely.

We played with Saleem again at the Weizmann Institute, this time without mishap. Saleem actually demonstrated a marked advance in confidence and fluidity. Surely this indicated not only his musical gift, but his resilient character and his plucky determination. A third performance with Saleem was boldly envisioned to take place in Nazareth. It would be Nazareth's first orchestral concert, and mark the inauguration of its new concert grand, the one Saleem had earned through his playing at the French Embassy. The Arab mayor had already pledged his attendance, and Maha had promised a home-cooked Arab meal for the entire orchestra. We were all looking forward to this event, even if it should cause a headache for the police to provide security. But alas, as it turned out, the event was not to be.

Spring 1994. Five years had passed, and the Nazareth concert with Saleem, which had eluded us back then, never materialized. The hoped-for piano from France did not arrive. Saleem moved on to new repertoire, and our orchestra to its own schedule. I became involved with immigrant musicians from the former USSR, who were arriving in the country by the hundreds. Worst of all, the *intifadah* kept escalating, and the deepening ethnic distrust transformed our Nazareth project into a naïve pipedream. It was, however, not only external conditions that hampered our project's realization. As time went on, Saleem's entire musical advance was put to the test. His willpower and his inborn talent–those two essentials in a young musician's development–were, in his case, not really sufficient. His remoteness from exposure to musical experience, from uninterrupted association with peers and competitors, began to be a debilitating handicap. Even more severe might be his inevitable departure from his own culture, so ill-timed in the increasingly nationalistic environment. Alone he sat there on the mountain, practicing, no longer a full member of his own world, and alas, not yet belonging to another. He was too young to decide his own destiny, yet too old to defer his choices any longer.

Many new questions arose. Saleem may well have outgrown his teacher, who worked mainly with beginners, and the chemistry between him and Valeria began to erode. He needed instruction in theory and harmony, but that was unavailable in his area. He needed to play chamber music, but no one else in Nazareth studied an instrument. If he should eventually succeed, would his detractors not protest political exploitation? And if he should not, would his supporters not contend ethnic discrimination?

I particularly remember a festive Christmas dinner at the home of Duaibis' mother, a tall matriarchal figure, dressed in black, who had been an English teacher in Nazareth in the time of the mandate. The whole family was there, sisters, cousins and children, and after the meal we all exchanged Christmas gifts. Then someone switched on the television, and the news showed, not surprisingly, clashes between stone-throwing Arab youngsters Saleem's age and Israeli armed soldiers, with casualties on both sides. The room fell silent. We suddenly felt, probably all of us, that we were play-acting in a fool's paradise, our freshly unwrapped presents in our hands. I did not go back to Nazareth for a long time.

We did not, however, drift apart. Maha's delicacies kept arriving, turning me into a veritable connoisseur of Arab cookery. One summer we went to France together, to a large music camp in the mountains, where Saleem quickly stood out among the pianists. And all through the Gulf War, while Iraqi Scuds fell on Tel-Aviv, the Abbouds phoned daily begging me to come and move in with them for the duration.

A few years went by before we vaguely began to make plans for another appearance of Saleem with our orchestra. By now he had grown into a tall, good-looking youth. He spoke fluent English and Hebrew. He was a regular participant at the Jerusalem Music Center master classes, and was often invited to take lessons with eminent pianists in Europe and in the USA. He had finally left the St. Joseph Seminary School in Nazareth for the Israel Arts and Science Academy in Jerusalem, a Hebrew-language boarding school for the exceptionally gifted. And he also acquired a new piano teacher, one of Israel's young and rising musicians, Eitan Globerson. Saleem's repertoire widened markedly, and one of his new objectives became the Tchaikovsky No. 1 Concerto, a major work by any standard.

And so we cooperated again, this time with Eitan's full knowledge and participation. When Saleem inadvertently raised his shoulder, Eitan would slap it down, and when he bent too much into the instrument, I would scream to re-establish contact. At the first rehearsal, orchestra members hardly recognized Saleem, so much had he grown in the intervening years. Again our rehearsal schedule had to be re-adjusted, this time because Saleem was sent on a US concert tour to raise funds for his school. There he also played for, and was introduced to, Prime Minister Yitzhak Rabin, on one of the latter's frequent visits to Washington DC.

We played the Tchaikovsky with Saleem five times in the main cities, to full houses and to much acclaim. Saleem had developed a brilliant technique and an intense, powerful presence. Our orchestra, too, had made great strides, and now included many well-trained immigrant players among its ranks. Yet our best performance, unquestionably, was the one in Nazareth, that long-awaited dream finally come true. Much like our previous attempt, the concert did not materialize smoothly. In spite of Duaibis' ceaseless efforts, two weeks before our scheduled date nothing was finalized, as hall after church were too booked to accommodate us. The mayor, too, regrettably had prior commitments. As a last resort Duaibis appealed to Father Emil, headmaster of the St. Joseph, Saleem's old school. Father Emil agreed at once, and within days, by word of mouth, the concert was sold out.

The event took place in the school's big hall, part church, part assembly. The concert grand, a full-sized instrument, was brought from Jerusalem for the occasion. The acoustics, partly church-like, were extraordinary. The stage area was well lit. Long before the start, the hall was packed beyond capacity, the audience expectant and proud. Finally a local poet read something in Arabic, and then it was as if those endless years of hard labor, of boundless sacrifice, of crossing the divide, were finally acknowledged. Saleem seemed more involved, even tense this time, and his performance more emotional. We too gave him a caring, spirited accompaniment. At the end there were cheers and flowers and curtain calls, surely and deservedly for Saleem, yet surely also for the evening's unspoken implications. In the refectory Father Emil, in black priestly robe, warmly greeted the orchestra, and Maha's long-promised meal for everyone proved well worth the wait. Then, next day, came the unexpected, auspicious, terrifying call. Mehta was in the country for a few days, and Saleem was to audition for him.

As often before, Saleem arrived at my house the night before, and we tried to spend a quiet evening, listening to Mozart. In the morning, joined by Eitan, we started out, three edgy clowns making silly jokes. Fifteen young soloists were there, and a small band of nervous parents and well-wishers. Saleem played last, the Tchaikovsky, of course. When he finished, Mehta spoke to him briefly, engaging him on the spot for a concert two weeks hence. On the way out, intercepted and questioned by the others, we pretended to know nothing, and went on. I took Eitan and Saleem to Fabio's for a hefty lunch, where we finally relaxed. Then Eitan took Saleem to catch a bus to Nazareth for one day's rest. After that, the two would have a busy time together. I liked Eitan. He was a true educator, and there was a superb camaraderie between him and Saleem. Eitan would make an excellent conductor, I mused, perhaps just the man to take over the Campus Orchestra one day. Turning to my own schedule ahead, I thought of little So-Ock Kim, the young Korean girl of eleven, who would soon arrive from London to play the Mozart Violin Concerto No. 3 on our next program. She had already appeared in Seoul, in Edinburgh, in Oslo, and at the Royal Festival Hall. And then I imagined how next week's Philharmonic concert announcement would probably read: The Israel Philharmonic Orchestra. Founded in 1936 by Bronislav Huberman. Music Director: Zubin Mehta. Laureate Conductor:

Leonard Bernstein. Honorary Guest Conductor: Kurt Masur. Zubin Mehta, conductor. Saleem Abboud, pianist. I smiled.

Summer 1995. We played with Saleem once more, at a kibbutz near Nazareth, to what became quite implausibly a mixed and friendly audience of Nazarene Arabs, Kibbutz members, and music enthusiasts from all over Israel. We did the Grieg A minor concerto, and Maha once again brought a rich, flavorsome Arab meal for the entire orchestra. That night, less than an hour's drive away, a particularly savage battle erupted between Palestinian demonstrators and Israeli forces. Our concert did not make it even into the news next morning.

Summer 2012. Saleem continued his studies at the Royal Academy in London with Maria Curcio, and at the Musik Hochschule in Hanover with Prof. Arie Vardi. He has worked closely with Daniel Barenboim, with whom he has performed in the world's major capitals. He has appeared with some of the world's major orchestras, such as the Chicago Symphony, the Berlin Staatskapelle, the Vienna Philharmonic, Milan's Filarmonica della Scala, and the Birmingham Symphony, with conductors Riccardo Muti, Lawrence Foster, Manfred Honeck, and others. He was invited to be on the board of the West-Eastern Divan Orchestra (the orchestra of Arab and Israeli young musicians founded by Daniel Barenboim and Edward Said), and has lately taken an interest in conducting. Now in his mid thirties, he is a sought-after soloist, recitalist, and chamber musician. He lives in Berlin, is married, and has twin daughters.

Saleem's younger brother Nabeel also became a musician, a violinist. He studied physics and music at Tel Aviv University, and later gained a master's degree at the Musik Hochschule in Rostock, Germany. He is a member of the West-Eastern Divan Orchestra, and with Barenboim's encouragement founded the Polyphony Conservatory in Nazareth, where he serves as director and head of the violin department. The Conservatory is home to Arab as well as Jewish youngsters in the region. In 2012 he was awarded in New York City the Yoko Ono Lennon Courage Award for the Arts. Nabeel lives in Nazareth and is also married.

In our land, peace remains as elusive and unachievable as ever. Yet the Abbouds and I are still the best of friends, bonded, I think, forever.

Saleem, a successful concert pianist, in Berlin
(Duaibis Abboud-Ashkar)

15

A Room with a View

Rio de Janeiro with Sugarloaf mountain beckoning

The Gloria Hotel is a large, old world edifice of elegance and tradition. It is early morning local time, though night for me biologically. Drawing the curtains open, I discover a haphazard fusion of curved bays and wide avenues, a random juxtaposition of ocean and mountains and, unmistakably, Sugar Loaf looming portentously in the distance. I wasn't aware that the hotel was so close to the sea when I arrived in the dark a few hours earlier. The view is breathtaking, and I immerse myself in it. Rio de Janeiro is unquestionably one of the most stunning cities anywhere. Something, in a flash, seems askew, though. The shadows of the rising sun are advancing in the wrong direction. I realize, of course, the sun is not mistaken, just we Northern Hemisphere dwellers are. On the pavement below, beachcombers sing merrily around a half-naked guitarist, and in the little patch of green across the street a loud football practice is taking place. What an enormous land, I ponder, what a lucky, war-less country, this Brazil—or as locally pronounced *Braziou*, *'ou'* replacing the letter *L* at the end of a word. Like *Rio de Janeiro, Distrito Federaou*. Funny, I conclude.

The distinction, of course, goes much deeper than the way the shadows move. Brazil is essentially European, but the abysmal gulf between rich and poor would not be tolerated in the West. On the other hand, Europe could only covet the painless mix of race, color, and religion. Ever since my previous visit here long ago, I have been struck by the local exuberance, the buoyancy, the sense of improvisation. In a way, I have throughout the decades tried to adopt some of these qualities myself, more in envy, though, than with success.

Even now I am slightly anxious. The first encounter with a new orchestra can be daunting, more so than the apprehension felt moments before the start of a concert. I like to arrive at a first rehearsal early and chat with the musicians as they turn up. It eases the tension, both ways. No use to march onto the stage triumphantly at the last moment, and expect instant rapport. I look at my watch.

Finally, the phone rings. I am gratified. Looks like I have not been forgotten.

"Hello?"

"Maestro?" says a woman's voice.

"Yes," I say cheerfully. I am no longer alone in this hemisphere.

"Allo, Maestro, good night."

Good night? How right she is, I reflect.

"Well, good morning," I say. In Rome do as the Romans do, I think.

"Ah, is correct, Maestro, is morning. Good morning, Maestro. Speaka da pianista, your soloist for concert."

"Well, hello." I know her name, of course, but not how to pronounce it.

"Maestro, I wiou pick-up you for your hoteou in ten hours. Okay, Maestro?"

It takes me a second to get accustomed to her accent.

"You mean at ten o'clock?"

"Yes, in ten hours o'clock."

Somehow, I am faintly mistrustful.

"At what time is the rehearsal?"

"Ten hours o'clock, Maestro."

"Well, maybe we should leave a bit earlier then?"

"Okay, Maestro, I come your hoteou nine thirty hours o'clock."

"That will be fine," I say, and as an afterthought, "Bring your score with you, okay?"

"Yes, I am take."

"All right then, thanks very much."

"Bye, Maestro, Chao."

I am much relieved. Now there is even time left for a quick breakfast. Walking to the elevator on my floor, I hear, incredibly, someone practicing the Mendelssohn Violin Concerto, superbly executed. Further down the corridor, the sound of a cellist playing a Brahms passage, just as accomplished. Curiosity gets the better of me, and the night-shift receptionist, luckily still on duty, divulges that it is the Berlin Staatskapelle with Daniel Barenboim on tour. I am awed and puzzled. Do the Brazilian players also practice before breakfast?

The Gloria breakfast hall is an equatorial dream. A huge glass wall reveals lush, tropical foliage outside, and pungent, exotic food generously laid out inside. I drink a glass of juice, and proceed to the lobby. Elegant Latin types in beige and white tailored suits fill the hall. An H. Stern stewardess, unerringly identifying new arrivals, offers free visits to the famous jewelry factory. I have already been handed this invitation at the airport, surprisingly even *before* passport control. Hesitantly, a gentle young woman approaches.

"Maestro?"

I nod, and she swings her arms around me and kisses me on both cheeks. It is, I gather, the Brazilian way of getting introduced. "The driver outside, Maestro," she informs me. Passing a band of saluting bellboys, we are helped into the vintage orchestra car.

On the way, the driver decides to take a short detour and show me a bit of Rio. To my utter bafflement, I don't object. The city's allure is irresistible, and I feel the rapport already. Wide sun-swept beaches, gracefully soaring palms, modern high-rises amidst crumbling colonial residences, and heroic statues of famous *libertadores* pass us as we gallivant merrily toward our destination. At the gate, the security man refuses to let me enter without my passport, which is at the hotel. A lengthy discussion between the driver and the sentry ensues, ending abruptly in loud laughter, signaling a friendly resolution, and we are allowed in.

By now the Petrobras Symphony Orchestra, is ready and tuned, and I must do what I like least–march on as a complete stranger, utter a short good morning, and give an upbeat. Indeed, the first sounds are not overly convincing. Is it the orchestra's level of competency, or the players' momentary unease? If I halt too soon, it may trigger indignation; but if I carry on too long, it may provoke indifference. Quickly I call for a stop, maintaining only that surely the players could do better. We start again, and instantly the sound improves and the rehearsal comes to life.

During intermission, the first cellist asks if I would have a bite with a group of players after the rehearsal. I agree willingly, and when the orchestra disperses I am taken to an eatery nearby and we all have spicy grilled chicken. The gentle soloist is Brazilian, a graduate of the National Conservatory. The cellist is an Italian from Guatemala, several newcomers are from Russia, one quiet young woman is a refugee from Bosnia, and one violinist, the assistant concertmaster, had spent a year on a kibbutz in Israel. The orchestra's driver is being released, and I am taken back to the hotel by a lady violinist who invites me to her family for a Rosh Hashana dinner the following week.

I grab a quick dip in the Gloria swimming pool and return to my room, to catch up on my jet-lag before a meeting with the orchestra administrator. The curtain is wide open, and the view through the window is as breathtaking as before. Sugarloaf beckons, and tomorrow after the rehearsal I shall be taken up there by the first cellist and the Bosnian refugee. The musicians' informality and their friendliness are captivating, and I feel good about our rehearsal tomorrow and the concert next week. *Braziou*, I find, is unquestionably infectious. The shadows, however, now almost in the other direction, are still all slanting the wrong way.

Rio, as I soon discovered, had a dark side to it as well: a very high incidence of violent crime. Behind the carefree façade, danger lurked. I was warned not to go out of the hotel by myself. My generous host, Music Director of the Petrobras Symphony Orchestra Armando Prazeres, was assaulted and robbed the night of my concert, while on his way home in one of the many tunnels cutting through the city. I left early the next morning without seeing him. As if this were not enough, his son Carlos wrote me soon afterwards that his father had been assaulted again, and this time, tragically, he had been shot dead.

Rio's enormous 'Cristo Redento' statue atop Corcovado mountain

16

A Passage to India

The Bombay Chamber Orchestra with pianist Dorel Golan,
Mumbai, 2002

India, for me, has always conjured up images of unfathomable mystery, of infinite patience, of ancient wisdom. There seems to linger, perhaps not just in my mind but in many a Westerner's who has never been there, a hidden urge to visit, as though in India time might perhaps miraculously come to a halt, or the riddle of human existence astonishingly find an explanation. An urge not unjustified, because of our obsession with constantly *doing* things, but also, precisely for the same reason, one that can be suppressed or postponed indefinitely. I had my doubts about ever making it to India.

What a surprise then, when one morning the fax machine at my home in Tel-Aviv issued forth an invitation to come to India practically right away, to replace a foreign conductor who had to cancel his commitment with the Bombay Chamber Orchestra, reputedly one of India's leading symphony ensembles. I was to propose the program and bring a soloist of my own choice. The temptation was of course irresistible. Within two hours I sent my acceptance.

We settled on Beethoven's Symphony No. 7 in A major as the central orchestral work, and on Verdi's Prelude to *La Traviata* as an opener. For our soloist I chose young Israeli pianist Dorel Golan, who requested to play the Schumann Concerto in A minor. A student of Prof. Vardi at Tel-Aviv University's Rubin Academy of Music, Dorel had already performed in various capitals abroad, and had played Beethoven's *Emperor* Concerto with me the previous season to great acclaim. Tessa would accompany me to India, play in the orchestra as flautist, and coach the wind section.

An extended flight through Addis Ababa landed us in Bombay, Mumbai nowadays, shortly after dark, and the first impact was overwhelming. Ripe, oppressive heat, huge and twisted trees sending their branches thirstily back to earth, myriads of rickety taxis and wobbly rickshaws scurrying in all directions sounding their horns relentlessly, and dense unending rows of families living in dark makeshift hovels along the long route to the city.

We finally arrived at the guesthouse of the National Centre for the Performing Arts, a large fenced-in and guarded compound facing the Arabian Sea at Nariman Point, Mumbai's prime business area. Here comfortable, air-conditioned quarters awaited us. A kindly, white-uniformed attendant, Mr. Shankar, welcomed us, and throughout our stay saw to all our domestic needs.

The white-haired lady who greeted me the next morning and led me to the rehearsal was Miss Jini Dinshaw, officially Joint Honorary Secretary of the Bombay Chamber Orchestra Society. She was the one who had invited me to India and had made all the arrangements. I had assumed her to be one of the orchestra's administrators, but it soon turned out she was much more than that. As a young violinist trained in England, it was she who, upon returning to India, founded the orchestra in 1962, serving as its coach and director these past forty years.

Light of structure and rather nimble, her face was shapely and expressive, and her eyes kind. It was her abundant white hair, contrasted against her olive complexion, that was so remarkable, and almost the only hint of what must have been her true age. When we reached the rehearsal hall, Miss Dinshaw introduced me to the members, and then, surprising me again, modestly took up her position in the last desk of the cello section.

I must confess that those first few seconds facing a new orchestra can be a bit awkward. Players are forever required to surrender their artistic ideals to the will of a stranger who, by authority or flattery or magic, must persuade them of the validity of his conception. Wariness and doubt may fill the air on either side. Also, it did not bolster my confidence to know that such luminaries as Lord Yehudi Menuhin, Walter Gieseking, Kendall Taylor, Nigel Kennedy, Piers Lane, and many others, had worked with this orchestra before me. The moment, however, passed without tension. Smiling faces, a friendly greeting, an unanticipated view of the Arabian sea through the glass behind the orchestra, and off we sailed together into the Beethoven.

Oddly, rehearsals were scheduled to start uncommonly early for a musician—at 7.00 am—and to last only one-and-a-half hours, half the length of a standard orchestra session, the reason being that all the orchestra members were volunteers, and had to hurry to work or to school as soon as the session was over.

Broadly speaking, there are three types of orchestras in the world: the full-time high-budget one, the part-time low-budget one, and the practically no-budget volunteer or 'community' one, in which instrumentalists play principally for their pleasure. What they all have in common, though, in widely varying degrees, is the need for funding, mostly institutional in the first case, regional in the second, and private in the third. Clearly, the musical standards will differ markedly between the categories, usually, sad to say, to the latter's inevitable disadvantage. Historically, though, many orchestras, including some of the world's most renowned ones, started out as volunteer ensembles. It could also be said that the enthusiasm and dedication of aficionado players are not always matched by their professional counterparts.

As I stood in front of the orchestra, there sat before me an eager group of players, some of whom had left home at 5.00 am, to be picked up at Bombay's central railway station at 6.30 am by none other than Jini Dinshaw in her car, and by her able assistant, the orchestra's timpanist Bomi Billimoria in his. As a rule, volunteer orchestras tend to rehearse normally once a week, perhaps twice before a concert. Here, astoundingly, was a volunteer ensemble willing to rehearse daily for a full three weeks, including Sundays. This, without doubt, was due to Jini's untiring and inspiring leadership.

An orchestra typically reflects its surrounding society. Here most players were Indian, yet some were Europeans, two brothers were half Lebanese, and one was a lady from Japan. There were Hindus, Parsees, Sikhs, Buddhists, Muslims, Christians and, with Tessa and myself, even Jews, and all, strikingly, played together in harmony. I also learnt that most of the members, especially the string players, had been Jini's pupils from the start.

Of course, as I soon discovered, there were better and weaker players, creating unevenness in execution. Some were able to maintain good eye contact with the conductor, but for others this was more difficult, causing the ensemble at times to fall apart. As in any volunteer orchestra, absenteeism, in spite of all good will, is almost unavoidable, and the occurrence of late-comers or early-leavers, an annoying yet inexorable impediment. One player in particular, a contrabassist, impressed me with his earnestness, yet more than once he would arrive a good half hour late, meticulously unpack his large and bulky instrument, participate attentively for ten or fifteen minutes, then look at his watch, quietly pack up, and tiptoe away.

Strangely, these inevitable hindrances, which in the West would be considered unacceptable, seemed only to heighten the orchestra's resolve. Before and after each rehearsal, every player would pitch in to arrange or clear the stage as needed. Jini herself, in her calm and modest way, was always first to arrive and last to leave.

I marveled at Jini's enterprise. Receiving no grants or subsidies from the authorities, the orchestra is forced to rely entirely on the generosity of private donors, friends, and advertisers. Thus, in addition to her musical duties, Jini has also been, since its inception, the orchestra's lobbyist, marketer, fund-raiser and, I suspect, financial backer. A collector of musical instruments, she has been providing instruments willingly to all those players who could not afford to possess their own.

Although our official working day ended before breakfast, impeccably served by the ever-present Mr. Shankar, Tessa and I did not become tourists right away for the rest of the day. Tessa was in high demand to coach the wind players and even their young pupils, and the guesthouse living room quickly became a busy conservatory for the length of our stay.

I too worked with some players individually, going through tricky solo passages or complex rhythmic phrases, and soon found myself to be a vigorous advocate for practicing with a metronome, that little tick tock device which keeps one playing to the beat. I must admit I was not too successful in this endeavor. In the West, unable perhaps to grasp the infinity of time, we are quite pleased to dissect it into tiny, precise, controllable bits. Here, where time seems to be perceived more in its unending, uninterrupted flow, breaking it up so rigidly might have much less of an appeal. Indeed, listening to traditional Indian music, I experience difficulty in identifying and following a beat, although I know very well that there must be one.

We did, however, besides making music, venture out into Bombay. One had only to cross the street to reach the modern, luxurious 'Oberoi Hotel,' where several of the orchestra musicians, dressed in white jackets and bow ties, were playing in the twenty-floor high lobby. Crossing the street was an adventure in itself, having to navigate precariously between hasty, over-confident, and uncharitable drivers on the one hand,

and alluring, playful, yet persistent little beggar-children on the other. Delightful were the many colors everywhere. Surely, the Indian *sari* is a woman's most flattering attire, diverse and vibrant, rich and enticing.

We also visited the famous *Elefanta* caves, an hour's boat ride from Bombay's grandiose and finely embellished 'Gateway to India,' a colonial monument erected a century ago on the occasion of the first Royal Visit from Buckingham, and now a major tourist attraction. The caves, evocative of the mysterious, unforgettable Marabar caves in E.M.Forster's *A Passage to India* (1924), are immense temples hewn into the mountainside, complete with intricate deities sculpted into the stone, dark water pools, menacing crows, and hungry, impudent monkeys.

The splendor and wealth of color can be found not only in the luscious fabrics the women wear, but on the dinner table as well. It would be vain for a novice like me to describe the endless variety of tastes and spices offered in Indian dishes. The startling hues and appealing shades in which food is served are enough to satisfy one's senses. Jini and Bomi went out of their way to offer us a glimpse of lush Indian cuisine. We had a succulent lunch at the exclusive 'Copper Chimney,' a choice Sunday brunch at the trendy 'Marine Plaza,' and a sumptuous dinner at the elegant, colonial 'Taj Mahal Hotel.'

A particularly friendly evening was spent at the home of Bomi Billimoria and his wife Anita, whose two children, who had received their initial musical education from Jini, were now grown and living abroad as professional musicians. With us at the dinner table, besides Jini, were two well-behaved young English-speaking children, "These are the children of our maid," Bomi explained after the maid, who had served the meal, had returned to the kitchen. "It would be impossible for her to meet the expense of an education for these youngsters, and without it, there would be no future for them whatsoever. So we have decided to provide their education." And when the meal was over, Anita said, "Now, children, go to the kitchen and help Mummy with the dishes." The noble mission Bomi and Anita had taken upon themselves, and the simple way in which it was explained, astounded us.

A very special visit was a luncheon at Jini's home. She resides in a sprawling, comfortable, and airy rooftop apartment in the city's central area. Most of her time she devotes to teaching music, and, if I understood her correctly, she does it all without remuneration. She has been doing this for most of her life, some of her pupils nowadays being the children and grandchildren of her early ones. Not all, however, continue to play their instruments, and quite a few of her former students have left the country for other lands. Once, in a moment of introspection, Jini told me emphatically, "When I am gone, Bomi will take over the orchestra."

Jini, as well as Bomi, are Parsees, or Zarathustrans, a small minority among the fifteen million inhabitants of Bombay. In showing us the city, Jini took us past the famous *Hanging Gardens* to a large walled-in tract of land belonging to the Parsee community, and explained its use. Parsees do not bury their dead, but leave the bodies in the open to disintegrate naturally. "Zarathustra was the first ecologist," she said.

A week before the concert, the English contingent arrived— eight or nine free-lance London musicians, mostly wind players, invited to reinforce the orchestra for our performance. The Bombay wind section was indeed a bit short handed, there being almost no qualified wind teachers in the city and, sadly, not a single music conservatory. This state of affairs indisputably thwarts the ensemble's potential to transform itself into an institutionalized body of homegrown musicians. I often wonder if the scarcity of public support for the cause of Western classical music is not a reflection of a broader, lingering refutation of colonial values.

The added players expanded the orchestra's sound at once, and enhanced its sonority. The Beethoven Symphony began to contain the power and the inevitability so essential for this work. The next day Dorel Golan arrived, and charmed everyone with her sensitive yet authoritative artistry. Tall and slim and twenty-one, she made the romantic Schumann come to life even when playing an upright for the two rehearsals before we moved onto the stage of the spacious, fan-shaped, famed US architect Philip Johnson's designed Tata Theatre.

Then came the big day. It was a Sunday, and we had a morning rehearsal, and met again an hour before the concert. I think no matter how many times one has gone out onto a stage, there is always an air of concerned expectancy, a strange mix of joy and anxiety, before the start. By now the *Tata*, with over a thousand seats, had filled up to capacity, the orchestra was seated and had finished tuning, and I was about to step out for the Verdi Prelude, content that all our preparations had gone so well.

Someone, anguished, pulled me back with the inopportune news that one of Dorel's heels had just broken off her shoe. Indeed, the Verdi being short, little time was left to extricate the poor girl from her ill-fated predicament. Unbeknown to the waiting audience, a delegation with the broken shoe was quickly dispatched outside the Centre's fence, where normally a multitude of fruit-vendors, cobblers, barbers, palm-readers, and healers, abound; but this being Sunday, the street was empty. I suggested that Dorel come on stage barefoot, or perhaps have the other heel broken off, but my proposals were vetoed. Eventually, as a charitable lady was about to offer Dorel her own shoes, I went off to do the Verdi.

The concert, by all accounts, was well received. Dorel was brought out for many a curtain call, and played two Chopin encores brilliantly. The Symphony too sounded better, I felt, than in any of our rehearsals, and I was proud to ask the players to rise repeatedly and acknowledge the applause. The most touching moment came when Jini agreed to come forward from her cello seat, to accept the respect and the love sent to her by everyone.

It is always sad when a concert is over, and one has to part from new-found friends. Our leave-taking from Mumbai was poignant. India, however, will remain in my consciousness as vividly joyous. I will remember with esteem that keen assemblage of dedicated musicians, and with deep admiration its white-haired initiator Jini Dinshaw, generous, compassionate, and unassuming.

In the intervening years, Tessa and I have kept in touch with Jini and the Billimorias, and have on several occasions sent them young Israeli soloists for their concerts. In 2012 the Bombay Chamber Orchestra celebrated its fiftieth year, with Jini, now in her eighties, presiding. The audience at the final concert, we were told, gave Jini a long and well-deserved standing ovation for her half-century of work.

Meanwhile, the Billimoria children have remained abroad, son Farhad as concertmaster of an orchestra in Germany, daughter Dilshad as a free-lance flautist in the USA. Of the foster children, Sweta, the older, recently graduated in philosophy, standing first in her college and third in Mumbai University. She wants to do something connected with women's rights, and she also plays in the cello section of the orchestra. Sumit, the younger one, is in his second year of an undergraduate degree in commerce. A computer wizard, he wants to do something in that field. He too loves music and plays in the orchestra percussion section, together with his benevolent foster father, the modest Bomi Billimoria.

Tessa's daily woodwind seminar

With loyal attendant Mr. Shankar

With Jini Dinshaw and Tessa

17

Brief Encounter

"Interviewer: 'Mr. Previn, how long do you
remember what you just conducted?'
Previn: 'Oh, about fifteen minutes.'
Such a genius and without self-importance or super ego!"
Marcel L'Esperance, friend and choirmaster, Tokyo, 2002

Returning home from South America, my flight was interrupted for a one-night stopover in London. The choice of what to do with a free evening in London was agonizing. The city has so much to offer, especially for someone living outside Europe. I should really stay a week, at least, and hear some music, I mused, but rehearsals waited for me at home the next day. Perusing the options, my eye caught an announcement of the London Symphony Orchestra playing a Beethoven program that evening, with Andre Previn, the LSO's music director, conducting.

Andre Previn! His name evoked vague and long-forgotten associations. Oddly, although he was world-renowned for half a century, I had never seen him conduct live. And here he was, doing the very symphony I had done the night before in one of South America's lesser capitals, with that country's aptly-named but ill-endowed *Orquesta Sinfonica Nacional*. If I could hear how this work, while still fresh in my mind, should really sound, and even more to the point, see how it should really be conducted, my evening would be complete. Miraculously, the Barbican had a spare ticket.

The concert was indeed perfect. Previn led with authority, yet with sensitivity and inspiration. His tempi, his *rubati*, his balance, were exactly as I would have wished them to be, nothing was exaggerated, nothing ignored. And the players, of course, were incredible. The intonation, the ease of execution, the togetherness, the subtle interplay between the orchestra and the maestro's slightest indications, were supreme. No need even to mention the Barbican's unmatched acoustics, its elegance, magnitude, and comfort. The inevitable comparison with what had gone on the night before made me cringe. Where did I get the audacity to do a Beethoven symphony, or, for that matter, to presume to conduct at all? And how could I have come with demands of any kind to those poor, grossly under-trained and scandalously under-paid musicians?

When the music ended I found myself drawn towards backstage, where I discovered the maestro in front of his dressing room, quietly receiving a small group of well-wishers. Almost diminutive of stature, bespectacled and slightly stooped, he looked much older than my image of him, older even than his appearance on stage minutes earlier, yet his eyes were clear and kind. I joined the queue, which moved briskly, and when my turn came, I whispered some polite words and turned to go. Previn looked at me, examined me closely, and said, "Do I know you?"

Of course he could not have remembered. It was so brief, and so long ago. "No," I replied, touched nevertheless by his attention, "it was just the music that made me come by." He still looked puzzled, and I felt a sudden urge to come clean. "I did attend one of your concerts," I said haltingly, "in Pasadena, some forty years ago." It was a silly thing to say, and I regretted it at once. Previn, however, astounded me. "Oh, I remember Pasadena," he said, ignoring the people waiting in line behind me. "You do?" I wondered aloud. Pasadena could not have been a very memorable event for him. "Your soloist was a young pianist, Valeska Drucker," I hastened to inform him, "She played the Cesar Franck Variations."

His eyes lit up. "Of course," he exclaimed, "Valeska Drucker." A weird sensation overcame me. It had been decades since I heard anyone pronounce her name. "I was present at all your rehearsals," I added by way of explanation, in case he thought he did recognize my face. Previn would have been twenty-five then, already well established as a Hollywood composer, and Valeska, about twenty. She had just returned from a year in Rome, where she had studied with two world-renowned musicians, Pianist Carlo Zecchi, and conductor Artur Rodzinski, who with his wife Halina regarded her almost as a daughter. As for me, a foreign student in California, I was about Previn's age, perhaps slightly older. "She was a fine pianist," he said amiably, and then more seriously, almost to himself, "I wonder what became of her."

I, of course, knew only too well. "I was dating her at the time," I said, "and that concert brought us together. Soon afterwards we actually got married." I had no intention of opening this Pandora's box of mine, but there it was. Previn was beside himself with delight. "Oh, you must give her my regards," he insisted, and embraced me warmly. His enthusiasm was overwhelming, and it took perhaps a fraction too long before I replied. "I cannot," I said, "she died many years ago."

He was visibly pained, embarrassed perhaps at his own display of gaiety. "I am so sorry," he said earnestly, embracing me again, more intimately this time. It was my turn, in a manner of speaking, to console him. "Actually," I allowed, "we were divorced long before she died."

He drew back. My clumsiness had been unpardonable. Unwitting as it was, I had dragged him into making a spectacle of himself in front of all those strangers. In truth, I was always uncomfortable with that chapter of my life, and guardedly reticent about it. But I did not regret having told him. He had been more instrumental in my marrying that girl than I had previously admitted, and it seemed to me now that I had fallen in love with her more perhaps for her music than for herself. From the little I knew about his own marriages (he was in his fourth at the time and in his fifth at the time of this writing), I could only hope he would understand my clumsiness.

Indeed, instead of terminating our interview, which he could have easily done, he continued with renewed interest. "So, you live in London now, or back in L.A.?" he asked. "Neither," I replied cheerfully, relieved that the previous subject was let go, "I live in Israel. I'm Israeli." We were, so to speak, brothers. He gave no sign of acknowledgement, and remained silent. Had I created yet another muddle in our bumpy discourse? Previn was not known much for his association with Israel, and the sudden allusion to what might be a sensitive issue may have upset him. He would have been about nine when his parents fled Germany for the USA, about the same age I was when mine escaped Europe for Palestine—old enough to remember. Tread softly, I cautioned myself, and I too said nothing. We may have stumbled upon another Pandora's box, this time his. But neither of us opened it.

"And what do you do?" he suddenly shot at me. Now it was my turn to be discomfited. How do you tell Previn that you do more or less what he does, in an infinitely more modest way of course, yet with perhaps no less dedication and contentment? I think he knew the answer almost before I spoke. Abruptly he grabbed my hand, shook it for an instant, issued a curt "Goodbye," and vanished into his dressing room, shutting the door behind him. The few admirers who were still waiting to see him pierced me with their angry looks.

I was mortified. Had he suspected me of being some clown or imposter, a deluded old failure perhaps, come begging for help or reinstatement? On the other hand, the extraordinary ease of backstage access, unwise really in our age, would require him to be mistrustful. Be this as it may, I came away unblemished: he had not asked for my name, and I had not disclosed it to him.

As I emerged into the street, the London night was pleasant. It was not raining, and I decided to walk back to the hotel. The symphony still rang in my ears, and I thought back to my concert the night before in the decaying, ill-ventilated, acoustically mute *Teatro Nacional*. In the middle of the second movement there was an electricity cut, and we waited motionless in the dark, drenched in perspiration, for what seemed an eternity. When the lights finally came on again, I was amazed to see the house as full as before, and at the end the audience gave us a standing ovation. The previous night, I had been invited for dinner at the home of one of the players. It was a one-room lean-to with a tin roof and earthen floor, stiflingly hot and mosquito-ridden. We had discussed music late into the night. The morning after the concert, during breakfast on the spacious poolside veranda of the bustling *El Presidente* Hotel, a high-ranking UN Peacekeeping officer in uniform suddenly stopped at my table. "That was a pretty good concert you did last night," he said with a pronounced Scandinavian accent. "We don't get many like that out here." Perhaps the symphony we had done was not that worthless, after all.

Valeska Drucker, however, was still on my mind. Sadly, with all her beauty, youth, and promise, she did not make a career. She was gentle and warm-hearted, but insecure and unpredictable. One day, a few years into our marriage, she just left. Drifting about, she stopped playing altogether and went into a succession of ill-fated marriages. Eventually, I was told, she died poor and sick somewhere in Italy.

When we parted, I was, truth to tell, angry and heart-broken. After that I never saw her again except once, some years later. Across the oceans she asked to see me, and when we met she begged for us to get together again. She still had that youthful, charming innocence about her, but her unsteadiness frightened me, and the magic for me had gone. I declined. I have never regretted this decision, but have often been haunted by the sight of her desperate helplessness, her agonized sobbing, as I walked, or rather extricated myself, away. To this day I secretly grieve for her.

I had reached the hotel. There was just enough time to collect my things and start out for the airport.

18

Emeritus Chamber

The Emeritus Chamber Orchestra (Kushner)

Over a friendly breakfast one morning in the summer of 2005 with Yaacov Mishori, formerly principal horn of the Israel Philharmonic Orchestra and a past member of its board, I asked him, somewhat innocently, "How many retired IPO members do you think would like to play symphonic repertoire together, just for pleasure?" The question was perhaps not entirely innocent. I pondered about those first-class musicians, forced at the peak of their capabilities at age sixty five into retirement and sudden redundancy. Mishori kept updated accounts of IPO retirees and knew just about every professional musician in the country. "I suppose we could find out," he said, and faxed me his lists. On my first try, almost ten IPO and four Jerusalem Symphony retirees responded favorably. Not enough to create an orchestra, but enough to pursue the idea further, which I did.

Not every retiree from an orchestra is eager to join an ensemble again, especially a voluntary one. Some seniors take temporary jobs in smaller orchestras, some turn to teaching or chamber music, and some pack up their instruments altogether. After a lifetime of surrendering their artistic integrity to the whims of itinerant chefs, the thought of submitting to yet another conductor may be anathema to some. Yet most of those we approached found it a pleasant idea to play familiar repertoire in a relaxed, informal environment. Indeed, some of the most sought-after musicians and music educators in the country committed to the project, as well as advanced players of the younger generation, and almost unwittingly an ensemble of quality came into being, albeit on a zero budget. Considering the recruits' high average age, the name Emeritus seemed appropriate for such a venture.

I must confess that the august troupe made me feel a bit like the *Sorcerer's Apprentice*. Would these players, used to a continuous parade of world-famous conductors, accept me as conductor and music director? The contrasting functions of conductor and music director can pose an added difficulty for the person who takes on both posts. Conducting, contrary to what the public sees, is a lonely occupation. No one is privy to the conductor's long toil in mastering a score. The music director, on the other hand, must be a social-minded executive, setting repertoire, inviting soloists, coordinating dates and venues. His need, above all, is a telephone.

Lacking a rehearsal hall for the first four years of our

existence, we were obliged to rehearse at home (in our living room, angry neighbors not withstanding), thus unintentionally but opportunely creating an atmosphere of friendliness and intimacy. In our fifth year, Emeritus was awarded a residency at the Levinsky College of Education in Tel-Aviv, where we now enjoy proper rehearsal facilities.

The Emeritus is neither professional nor amateur, or alternatively, it is both. Operating without subsidy and performing for free, it is by definition an amateur enterprise. But because of the eminence of many of its players, it cannot be called amateur. A well-known Italian guitarist and conductor friend, Paolo Pilia, said to me in wonderment, "In Italy you would not find one musician willing to play for free after retiring from an orchestra." Yet world-class violinist Menahem Breuer, retired concertmaster of the Israel Philharmonic and occasional leader of the Emeritus, says, "I do this with pleasure. All the players seem to like this mutual music-making, which is a nice thing in itself."

In its short but active history, Emeritus has played to full houses not only in its regular concert series in Tel-Aviv, but also in unconventional venues such as the municipal community center in Ancient Nazareth, and the Protea Village auditorium in Tel-Mond. We have collaborated with leading educational music institutions, among them the Keshet Eilon music center, the Acre conservatory, the Maxim Vengerov music project, the Orpheus Music Association, and the Herzliya Gordon School of the Arts. Soloists and conductors who have appeared with the orchestra are well-established artists, as well as gifted young newcomers. Guest artists have included musicians from Belgium, China, Cyprus, Ecuador, France, Holland, Switzerland, Turkey, and the U.K.

Conscious of music's social and ethical obligations, the orchestra has presented young Arab soloists, such as pianists Fahdi Deeb and Nizar el Khater, and has played for Arab audiences. We undertook a charity concert in aid of the 2009 El Salvador flood victims, and celebrated the founding of Israel's first youth symphony, the Gadna orchestra, with quite a number of the original members participating. Abroad, the orchestra opened the Twelfth Bellapais International Music Festival in Cyprus with two demanding Beethoven programs, to warm public acclaim.

Comprising over forty players, the ensemble constitutes a full and well-balanced chamber orchestra, and usually prepares three to four programs per season. The works performed are among the best-loved of the classical repertoire, centered on Haydn, Mozart, and Beethoven. Habitually, the orchestra also introduces debut works of young composers. Ayala Asherov-Kalus, Yael Levi, and Cypriot Asli Giray, are among those.

One of our violinists, Prof. Menachem Shapiro, a semi-retired endocrinologist whose parents came to the USA from Russia when he was two, says, "My mother, who was a doctor, wanted me to be a violinist when I was a child, saying, 'Any idiot can be a doctor, but you have to be special to play violin.' So I started learning violin at age ten. My mother could not foresee that this would be the factor leading to my courtship and marriage to Judy, who is a talented pianist. We played duets on our first date and it was a 'closed case' between us. We moved to Israel several years later with three children and two more came along. Playing a musical instrument is part of the lives of all our children. They have all married and now their children are learning instruments; the 'disease' is being passed down. Playing violin is my 'morphine.' Playing with highly talented instrumentalists in our orchestra is like being in Gan Eden in this world."

Yet why would experienced professionals be eager to play with amateurs? Simply because retired pros are not always around to fill every position required, and in music, if one's orchestral set-up is incomplete, one does not play at all. Pros are thus willing to stretch their magnanimity, helping and instructing their less experienced peers, and attending more rehearsals than they would otherwise need. The fear, however, of violating this precarious balance between the two groups can cause a music director sleepless nights. What if the pros' patience runs out or if a pro is forced to quit?

Professional orchestra playing is a distinct specialization in music. In no way do I dismiss our non-professionals as inferior in enthusiasm and commitment, but clearly they don't have the experience the pros have. Our assistant concertmaster Nehama Rosler, who had joined the Jerusalem Symphony at age eighteen, took early retirement after thirty seven years. Our solo cellist Naomi Enoch retired from the IPO after thirty four years. Zvi Segal, IPO first violin, was in the Philharmonic for forty one years. Cellist Gershon Bar-On, a Bucharest music academy graduate, played in the Jerusalem Symphony for thirty eight years. First oboist Ehud Avichail stayed with the Jerusalem Symphony for forty years. Los Angeles born Richard Lesser, graduate of Philadelphia's Curtis Institute and the doyen of clarinet players in Israel, came to the IPO in 1967 as principal and stayed on for thirty four years. Yaacov Mishori, the celebrated horn player, author, and broadcaster, presenter of our concerts and irrepressible jokester, was an IPO member for thirty eight years.

This wealth of experience is not to be taken lightly. I

remember an IPO concert many years ago, in which Isaac Stern played a violin concerto, as usual to great acclaim. After the intermission, dressed in a light gray business suit, fiddle in hand, he tiptoed onto the stage, sat shyly in the last desk of the second violin section, and studiously played in the orchestra for the rest of the evening.

Pros have an obvious lead over aficionados in technical proficiency, familiarity with the repertoire, and most likely ownership of a superior instrument, but their primary advantage is the ability, while playing, to watch and follow the conductor, the key to the orchestra playing together.

I learnt of this perplexing duality early in life. As a teen piano pupil in the beginning years of WW2, I was invited to join a youth orchestra, organized by the newly arrived and well-known Czech conductor Georg Singer. The piano not being an orchestral instrument, it was decided that I should quickly learn to play the timpani, which I looked forward to with great excitement. I knew and admired the two boys who sat in the orchestra's first desk: Shimon Mishori, future concertmaster of the Jerusalem Symphony, and Haim Taub, future concertmaster of the Israel Philharmonic and world-renowned violin pedagogue. No one, however, explained to me how crucial it would be to watch the conductor, and the kettle-drum being a particularly loud instrument, every strike, especially if slightly off the beat, was instantly noticed by all. I saved my honor, eventually, when I discovered the trick, and from then on made sure to look at the conductor before every entry.

Actually, not much came of my episode as a timpanist in those days. Firstly, I didn't get to play much, as I was only assistant timpanist, the chief timpanist being a piano-playing girl a year older. I came to rehearsals regularly hoping she'd be absent, but that hardly ever happened. Secondly, I didn't get to practice much either. My teacher, IPO timpanist Kurt Sommerfeld, arranged for me to take two discarded timps home for practice. When the instruments arrived one afternoon, I waited patiently for my mother to leave the house, and started drumming. This took place only weeks after Italian airplanes had bombarded Tel-Aviv, causing damage and casualties. Not five minutes into my practice session, I heard our good neighbor Mrs. Greengart in the next building shouting my name across the balconies, ordering me down at once to the so called air-raid shelter at the building's entrance. There I was surprised to find almost all the tenants, visibly agitated, even angry at me for coming down so late. "But there was no alarm," I protested. "Be quiet," I was told, "There was no alarm. This is another air strike. Didn't you hear the bombs falling just now?" Only then did it dawn on me what, or more precisely who, had caused the mayhem. That, needless to say, was the end of my timpani career. The lesson, however, of having to watch the conductor relentlessly has not been forgotten.

Alan Tschaikov, a graduate of London's Royal College of Music, was Jerusalem Symphony's clarinet and bass-clarinet for forty one years. "I started playing the clarinet with my father," says Alan, "who was sub-principal clarinet in the BBC Symphony Orchestra. I did my National Service in the central band of the Royal Air Force. After a few years of freelancing I came to Israel in 1957 with my wife Maureen and a one-month old daughter, and joined the Jerusalem Symphony, having got the job already in England. Since retiring I have continued to teach and play chamber music, and together with Maureen, a pianist, musicologist, and librarian at the Jerusalem Academy of Music and Dance, we donate concerts to retirement homes. We have four married children. Our daughter is a nurse in a border kibbutz, and one of our sons is the commanding police officer in the Old City of Jerusalem. A curious coincidence is that my uncle Anton, a violinist who came here with the British Army during WW1, founded in 1919 a music school in Jerusalem, under the patronage of the celebrated diplomat, author, supporter of the arts, and Jerusalem Governor Sir Ronald Storrs. There Uncle Anton met and played chamber music with the noted cellist and music pioneer Thelma Yellin, who was a cousin of Maureen years before we were thought of."

Although the orchestra's nucleus derives almost exclusively from the two leading Israeli orchestras, Emeritus has an undeniable international flavor. Second violin principal Nora Amkhanitzky played for twenty years in the Armenia Chamber Orchestra in Yerevan. Russian violist Ida Kushner came from the Samara Philharmonic. Ukrainian Irena Baskin taught violin in Odessa. Latvian violinist Zena Perchekov retired from the Liege Opera after thirty two years. Israeli-born Dorit Lichtenstern of the London Royal Philharmonic was viola principal in the Dutch Radio Orchestra and the Sadler's Wells Royal Ballet. Sam Lewis, a conductor of musicals in England, played viola in the London Symphony Orchestra in his youth, and Canadian cellist Ari Kernerman, now a successful publisher of dictionaries in Israel, was Toronto Symphony's youngest member sixty years ago. Violinist Ariela Megiddo, wife of an Israeli career diplomat, was a member of the Bonn and the Washington DC chamber orchestras when her husband was posted there. Flautist Dafni Ben-Ozer, director of the highly regarded Givatayim conservatory, got her artist diploma from Indiana University. And flautist Tessa, besides being the orchestra's dedicated administrator, is a graduate of London's Guildhall School of Music

One of the dilemmas a music director constantly faces is the number of rehearsals to be allotted to a concert program. Too few, and the hoped-for quality is not achieved. Too many, and the excitement, the inspiration, is bound to wane. Altogether, too much orchestra activity may scare members away. Too little, and the group may never coalesce into a vibrant unit.

As befits a Jewish orchestra, Emeritus has its share of doctors and lawyers. Besides our endocrinologist Prof. Shapiro, we have among our ranks leading pediatrician Prof. Basil Porter of Ben-Gurion University, and dental surgeon Prof. Yakir Anavi of Tel-Aviv University. Attorney and violinist Abraham Dotan has played in every conceivable ensemble, including a mandolin orchestra, and attorney Shabtay Levy, whose musician father founded the Hadera conservatory, remembers how the Gadna orchestra was first initiated in his parents' home.

A new recruit who joined Emeritus is Donovan Bullen, an easy-going young Canadian. "I started playing electric bass in grade eight, and then picked up the contrabass in high school. Canada has some fine music programs, and I ended up going to the University of Western Ontario, where I received a Bachelor of Music, with honors in theory and composition. I also studied at Humber College for a year, basking in the guidance of some of Canada's finest jazz players. During this time, my girlfriend got a job at the Canadian Ministry of Foreign Affairs, and was sent on her first diplomatic posting to Israel. As my year ended at Humber, I decided to take some time off formal schooling and focus on practicing and private study. After some debate, I decided Tel Aviv was as good a place as any to do this. Currently, I am absolutely loving my time in Tel Aviv. I am practicing more and with greater focus than I ever have, and I feel my playing is reflecting this dedication. Furthermore, I have regular lessons with IPO bass player Eli Magen, who is a wonderful teacher. I have met several people in the local jazz scene and regularly attend jam sessions; my girlfriend and I are very happy together, and of course I have the pleasure of playing with Emeritus."

Perhaps the most unexpected members of the orchestra are two of our trumpet players, Uzi Eilam and Jacob Perry. Both are former generals of the Israel Defense Forces. Eilam was head of Israel's Atomic Energy Commission, and his recently published autobiography has become a best-seller (*Eilam's Arc,* Sussex Academic Press, Brighton-Portland-Toronto, 2011). Perry, former head of General Security, became chairman of one of the country's major banks, and has just recently won a seat in the *Knesset,* Israel's Parliament. Both men have played the trumpet since boyhood and relish their orchestra activity, at times delighting audiences with an unsolicited yet well-coordinated bugle call.

On one occasion Eilam managed to combine his military activity with his trumpet playing. In the offensive on Jerusalem's Old City during the 1967 Six Day War, Eilam (a Major at the time) and his battalion were the first to reach Judaism's holiest shrine, the Western Wall. Eilam was soon joined by IDF Chief Rabbi Shlomo Goren, whose function was to blow the traditional *shofar,* a ram's horn, to commemorate the victory. The Rabbi was so overcome by the momentous event, however, that no sound emanated from the ceremonial instrument he was holding to his mouth. "Give me the *shofar,*" suggested Eilam, "I'll blow it till you catch your breath." "You know how to blow a *shofar*?" inquired Goren. "No," answered Eilam," but I do play the trumpet." Whereupon Goren handed him the *shofar,* and

Eilam honored the historic moment until Goren regained his composure.

Inevitably, an assembly including members of advanced age is likely to experience early retirement, and suffer sad departures. Three former members of the IPO, violinists Henry Brender and Nathan Greenberg, and violist Ami Alroy, retired from Emeritus due to advanced age. Ze'ev Steinberg, IPO violist for almost fifty years, and surely the most energetic member of Emeritus, passed away recently at age ninety three. Composer, teacher of viola and chamber music at the Buchman-Mehta School of Music, jurist at the America-Israel Cultural Foundation and the International Harp Competition, and member of many ensembles, including the Israel Quartet, he is fondly remembered as Israel's veteran "Mr. Music." In a sequence of fate reminiscent of the Book of Job, only several weeks later our much-loved concertmaster Raffi Markus succumbed to illness. A London Guildhall graduate, Raffi joined the IPO in 1958 in the first violin section, a post he held for thirty six years until his retirement. A long-time member of the Israel Quartet, he performed in Israel, Europe, and Japan, and joined Emeritus at its founding. Like Ze'ev, Raffi was born in Germany, and the two were probably the last of the formidable generation of musicians who had originally come from that country.

Ze'ev's successor as Emeritus' viola principal is Yeheskell Beinisch, a lawyer-musician, former chair of the Jerusalem Symphony Orchestra, and currently chair of the Jerusalem International Chamber Music Festival and of the Jerusalem Academy of Music and Dance. Our concerts now regularly provide a musical education for the bodyguards of Yeheskell's wife, Israel High Court Chief Justice Dorit Beinisch, who has become a fervent Emeritus groupie.

Sam Zebba

Emeritus has turned out to be a closely-knit, jovial, and committed group, able to attract first-class artists and enthusiastic audiences. Do come and hear us, perhaps even join us if you play an instrument. samzebba@netvision.net.il.

Mishori introduces Emeritus concerts with humor and aplomb (D. Swade)

And I follow with eagerness, delight, and fascination (Aviram)

19

Epilogue

My life and education, my health, and probably my curiosity and optimistic outlook I owe to my parents. I have considered myself lucky to be their son, although I have taken a different route in life than they. Also, they were of quite dissimilar character from each other, and I have often wondered to whom I became more alike in nature. My father was more the extravert and a man of compromise, my mother more the introvert and a person of principle. I think I inherited something of both. I think also that my parents were not fully aware that I was happy doing what I did, and although they both lived reasonably long lives, I fear they did not realize that I had achieved a measure of contentment quite commensurate with my expectations. Now, nearing ninety, and almost at the stage of looking back, I can say without reservation that I have loved every minute of my sojourn on this planet.

20

My Epitaph

A would-be conductor next door
Could hardly decipher a score,
But in places afar
He became quite a star,
Such as Mumbai or San Salvador